Written Letters

33 ALPHABETS FOR CALLIGRAPHERS

written out by Jacqueline Svaren

TAPLINGER PUBLISHING COMPANY
New York

DEDICATED TO ALL STUDENTS

SECOND REVISED EDITION

Published in 1986 by

TAPLINGER PUBLISHING COMPANY

New York, New York

Copyright © 1975 by Jacqueline Svaren

All rights reserved

Printed in the United States of America

Library of Congress Catalog Card Number: 81-86266

ISBN 0-8008-8735-2

Dear Fellow Calligraphy Student

It is important that you know some things about this book before you begin to use it. To start with: the alphabets you find here are my INTERPRETATIONS of the real alphabets. They are presented here with the hope that you may find some of my methods & comments helpful in making your own discoveries about the letters. You should certainly have some clear facsimiles at hand, because you must become familiar with the real letters as they were written in their time in history. You will make your own interpretations based upon, if possible, the actual writing or, lacking that, good photographs (or "facsimiles"). A reasonably priced yet very beautiful & thorough little book of photographs of historic alphabets is Alfred Fairbank's A BOOK OF SCRIPTS published by Faber & Faber, Ltd. A bit more expensive, but certainly worth every penny is the catalogue to the 1965 Calligraphy Show in Baltimore titled 2,000 YEARS OF CALLIGRAPHY published by Rowman & Littlefield. Yet another very valuable book to have when researching the historical letters is by Herman Degering titled simply LETTERING & recently reprinted by Pentalic*. Reprinted by Ares Pub. is the extensive & scholarly INTRODUCTION TO GREEK & LATIN PALAEOGRAPHY by Maunde Thompson. There are, of course, many more fine books. Most of them, however, are quite specialized. It would indeed be a mistake to work from this little book believing the examples in any way adequate to replace the historical models. Please use my models as learning aids. They are meant to be reminders & facilitators. Perhaps in a few more lifetimes I may be able to write all (or some, or maybe ONE) of these alphabets flawlessly. I doubt it. So this book, if it is to exist, must be full of imperfections. Please overlook them, or, better still, BUILD ON THEM & learn from them.

Some suggestions for beginners have been included in this revised edition of WRITTEN LETTERS. There are

* TAPLINGER

iij

several excellent books which cover the beginnings in greater detail. Lloyd Reynold's ITALIC CALLIGRAPHY & HANDWRITING, published by Pentalic will be very helpful as will Alfred Fairbank's A HANDWRITING MANUAL published by Faber & Faber. Another beautiful helper is Edward Johnston's FORMAL PENMANSHIP edited by Heather Child & published by Taplinger/Pentalic.

So here we have an exercise book which contains examples of many of the most useful calligraphic alphabets. These examples appear the actual size they were written & without alterations (this means NO REDUCTIONS & NO WHITE PAINT.)* Therefore, these letters are all humanly possible instead of inhumanly perfect. Each alphabet is written with a small pen to give you an idea of how it looks in a mass as well as with a large (C-2 Speedball) nib to provide a clear working model complete with directional arrows &, I hope, helpful hints for execution. I have noted for you on each page the name & size of the pen used so you can use the same pen

when you write. It is very helpful to have models the same size as your own work. This page was written with a Wm Mitchell Roundhand No. 4. The tiny red writing throughout was done with a clipped crow quill pen.

I owe thanks to many people without whom I would never have attempted this book. First, to my parents, Jack & Thelma Moore, who have unfailingly encouraged me in all my endeavors. Then to my teacher, Lloyd Reynolds, whose dedication to beautiful letters & to the betterment of the human condition is a constant inspiration. His huge fund of shared knowledge has made any such attempt on my part possible. To my wonderful, understanding husband, Russell, & my very beautiful children Lynn, Jo Ann, Eric & Kelly, whose cooperation was essential. A special thanks to Thea Wheelwright for her uncompromising faith in the project. And, finally, to my students, especially my advanced students, who for years insisted that this book be done.

*Space requirements for this edition have forced the reduction of all the text areas except those on handwriting. None of the models or examples have been reduced. J.S.

Table of Contents

Written actual size with a clipped Crowquill pen.

TO BEGIN you will find it most helpful to understand some of the terms used in this book. Most calligraphers agree on general terminology, although we may find we disagree when it comes to materials &/or methods. Each teacher can only suggest those ways of working which for that person have proved the most satisfactory. You will no doubt find it desirable to experiment with many various approaches. My suggestions are just suggestions. They are not laws. They have, however, proved very useful to hundreds of students over the past 25 years.

FIRST, THE TOOLS: A speedball c-2 pen nib, or point, is recommended for several reasons. It is easily obtainable, (a quill is doubtless nicer, but ...) once broken in, it functions well, (break it in by clean^ing it either by dipping it^in ink & wiping it dry several times or by putting it in yr. mouth for a moment. You must do this with every new nib to remove the protective coating put there by the pen maker.) it is of a size consistent with the models in this book. It is much easier to learn letterforms if you use the same size nib as was used for your model. For a pen holder, use plain plastic or highly lacquered wood such as L&C Hardmuth. No cork, please. It gets dirty & causes smudges.

For ink, Higgin's Eternal is not as good as it once was, but it is better than most. Avoid India or waterproof inks. The best is probably Chinese sumi ink. My students use Nekoosa bond paper, from Blake, Moffit & Towne. I suggest a large sheet when working with a large pen. We use 17 x 22" tablets. Keep several extra sheets under your writing sheet for padding. Always protect the surface of the paper by keeping a piece of paper under your writing hand. A sloped writing surface is essential! Find an inexpensive drafting table or simply prop a drawing board up in yr. lap. 45° of tilt to the table will allow your spine to stay straight & your eyes to see what's happening on the page free from the inevitable distortions which take place unless your work is directly in front of & parallel to them. Get in the habit of always adjusting the paper so you write consistently in about a two inch square just in front of your nose. You will need a soft, absorbant piece of cloth to wipe excess ink from the top of your nib & to wipe the accumulated sizing off the tip now & then. Lastly, a 2H pencil & a 24" T-bar, or square with which to draw guide lines on your paper. Until you know the alphabet by heart you should have lines on every page. Once you've learned the letters, you can eliminate guide lines, or use a slip sheet under your page. The slip sheet has guide lines on it which show through your paper.

GUIDE LINES are determined by the width of your nib & the requirements of the alphabet. Holding your pen so the square tip is parallel to the edge of the paper make a mark without pressure on the nib. (Pressure spreads the tip so you don't get a true pen width. Pressure will also exhaust your hand & ruin the letters. Some forms require pressure, but generally you will want to maintain a very light touch.) Each alphabet in this book shows at the start how many pen widths are between the lines. i.e. } 3 pen widths Make a little ruler on a separate piece of paper & use it to indicate the distances between guide lines on your writing sheet. Use T-square & hard pencil to put the lines on your paper. (O! how I wish I were there to show you! Books cannot replace teachers.) Leave some margins. Every important thing deserves a margin, & you will never work on a more important sheet than this one. There is no such thing as "just a practice sheet." Each page you write on deserves your best, full attention. Now that your paper is accurately ruled, you are ready to establish the pen- or edge-angle.

THE PEN ANGLE is determined by the relationship of the tip of the pen to the horizontal guide lines. How you hold the pen will determine its angle. The letter forms depend directly upon the pen angle. Where the thicks & thins occur depends directly upon the pen angle:

nnnnnn

Play with your pen until you understand this basic principle. Then choose one angle & maintain it for a full page. It is essential that you can do this. Moving the writing sheet to keep the work directly in front of you will help a lot. Avoid holding the pen too tight. It is your best friend don't choke it! Exhale your strokes.

CHOOSE A MODEL. I recommend italic, Johnston's Foundational or Humanist Bookhand. Stay with it until you are comfortable with it. Switching about too soon will confuse & frustrate you. Pay as much attention to the white spaces, the counters, as to the black line which surrounds them. Trace a lot! Writing is a matter of kinetic imagery. Help the hand learn where to go. Just as in learning any skill you should practice every day. Find a good teacher as soon as you can. Good luck!

Of all the amazing things achieved by the Ancient Romans, the perfecting of the Majuscule Letters is the least often mentioned. Every school child knows of the aqua ducts & gladiators, but few associate the letters which surround them every day with the Romans. The TRAJAN COLUMN, erected in the 2nd century A.D. is the epitome of the classical Roman Letter in its inscription. We are unfortunately unable to study the inscription closely because of its inaccessible position. The great work done by Father E. Catich in his series of books has made close examination of the letters possible. Before getting too involved in the pen made letters it would be very fine if you could study the brush made then incised letters. They are made available for you in THE TRAJAN INSCRIPTION & THE ORIGIN OF THE SERIF, both by E. Catich.

The models offered here for a pen written version of the Roman Majuscule are much more practical. According to Sir E.M. Thompson in his fabulous INTRODUCTION TO GREEK & LATIN PALEOGRAPHY there are only two extant examples of books written in the square caps. One is divided between Berlin & the Vatican (this is the one I've seen) & the other is in St. Gall, Switzerland. There is a little bit of both in the example offered here. Working from the photographs in H. Degering's book LETTERING, I have formed this composit for you. You may want to examine my sources for yourself. I hope so! The following are from St. Gall: E, F, R, O, Q, L, Y. From the Berlin manuscript: B, C, D, M, N, R, S, X. Combined forms: A, G, P, T, V. & some I've invented for lack of an example on either historical sheet: J, K, U, W, Z.

A PEN MADE VERSION OF THE ROMAN MAJUS CULES KNOWN AS THE CAPITALIS QUADRATA

No one should try to write the inscriptional Caps with a pen - unless you happen to be a nut like me, who tries & tries for whatever understanding you may gain - rather than for the success you might hope to have. I feel that the hours & hours I spent trying to do those impossible letters with a pen served me well.

After you think you "have" them, ask someone who really knows how to write them for you with a brush - & try it yourself. (The brush is a marvelous tool every calligrapher should know how to use.) Then you will BEGIN to understand about the Roman Majuscules. No matter how long you work on them, they will always remain an idea - a hope - a goal.

Although I have done no retouching on any of the letters in this book, I have chosen the best of a pageful & cut & pasted.

The way you breathe as you write is important. EXHALE the strokes. Holding your breath will make the letters stiff & self-conscious.

Strive for equal amounts of space between letters, but delight in your humanity! Machines can measure; but they can't invent.

Think of the Roman Majuscules as architecture! Just as the Colosseum & the Pantheon, they need plenty of space around them.

The Square Caps were written with a Wm Mitchell Roundhand No. 2 nib.

4 pen widths high

A — The main pen angle is quite flat. The nib is held almost parallel to the guide lines. Pen angle must be steepend for the thin strokes such as no. 1 on A.

Go up on the left corner of the nib to draw the foot.

B — The center of B need not close.

Build the foot to the left.

C — Overlap the first stroke with the second to avoid a weak spot.

Up on the left hand corner of the nib for the top serif & up on the right for the bottom

Let the pen angle vary slightly. (You are dancing, not goose-stepping!)

D — Learn to watch the counters as you write.

The counters are the white spaces you form as you make the black lines.

E — About a 5° pen angle for the little horizontals.

Be sure 3 & 4 are the same length.

With a smaller nib you may simplify the serifs on E, F. See p.3

The bottom of E is a little longer.

F — Draw the serifs as on C.

Such an almost flat pen angle for the foot.

G — Please center the jaw on G.

Not a bull dog G or a c-clamp G

H — Move your whole torso as you form the horizontal. Rock to the right.

I — EXHALE THE STROKES.

Be sure the writing is in front of you & your paper is straight.

A SLOPED WRITING SURFACE IS ESSENTIAL!

L — Use right corner of nib

M — Let it be wide!

Turn the nib to form the middle point.

N — Fill in this corner

Very steep p.a. for 1 & 5

Turn the nib to 90° to form this corner. (Let your elbow move out to the right to achieve 90°)

O — OVERLAP!

The inside counter is more a fat lemon than a tennis ball.

OVERLAP!

P — Spring up from the stem, allowing a SLIGHT depression to form in the top silhouette.

You may close P if you want. This seems very elegant to me.

Q — close it strongly.

R — This is the Berlin R which seems too strange to many people.

The St. Gall R is more familiar.

Both R's grow the beard out of the chin of the upper lobe.

S — Use a steeper pen angle for the middle of S.

Draw the serifs.

Left corner of nib

T — Because a long horizontal is so difficult to control, I've left it short as in the Berlin version. You may want to make it longer.

V — Turn the nib to form the point.

X — Make X of 2 straight strokes. Curves cause trouble.

Draw.

Y — This Y looks like the Greek upsilon.

Y — This is a modern version.

Z — The terminations are drawn. Keep Z dignified.

J — The Romans had no J, so we have no model. You might want to experiment with it.

Retracing here helps.

K — Try for a 90° angle on this counter.

U — Though NOT a truly historical form, thus it is strong & seems to fit.

W — 1 & 3 are parallel 2 & 5 are parallel destroying the myth that W is M up-side down.

Create points by manipulating pen angle.

LJR thoughout the book refers to my teacher, Lloyd J. Reynolds.

p.a. means pen angle.

Rustic as a bookhand is somewhat more flexible than Capitalis Quadrata.

It appears very beautifully & formally in the 5th cen. texts of VIRGIL. More commonly, & much more freely, it dances as a brush letter on the walls of ancient Pompeii. There it functions as a "commercial" letter-perhaps selling bread & extolling politicians.

One translation pleas: IF YOU WANT TO LEAN ON A WALL, PLEASE LEAN ON SOMEONE ELSE'S.

I do not recommend the use of this very difficult letter. However, I feel strongly that any serious student of letters should know it. You should understand it clearly before attempting the more useful, more attractive, & MORE DECEPTIVE Square Rustics.

Practice, practice!

THE RUSTIC ALPHABET OF THE 4TH OR 5TH CENTURY REQUIRES A VERY STEEP PEN ANGLE · IT IS HIGH WAISTED AND NARROW · TRY IT BEFORE YOU TACKLE THE MORE MODERN VERSION · USE A VERY RIGID NIB · TWIST THE NIB FROM 85° TO 50° TO SHAPE THE VERTICAL · USE ABOUT 50° FOR THE CURVED STROKES ·

"THE ONLY WAY TO STUDY LETTERS IS WITH A PEN IN YOUR HAND!" LJR

This page of Rustic was written with the Wm Mitchell cursive nib no. 7.

Wax tablets still exist showing the "common cursive script" which helped influence the development of Rustic. These wax tablets were the original "magic slates." They were usually made of wood covered by a thin layer of wax. The writing was accomplished by scratching thru the wax with a stylus - or pointed tool - so the wood showed through. Melting the wax made the slate usable over & over.

I find the spelling both ways: Vergil (B Catich) & Virgil (A Fairbank)

Overlap the top of A

The steep pen angle designs the letters & explains the droop of the bowls

1 7½ pen widths

Very steep pen angle

Slight concavity on both sides

Overlap

Watch the counter shape & size. You are lost if you see only the black line.

Start with a twist from a steep pen angle to a flatter one.

You might try holding the pen holder more vertically - as a brush would be held to achieve more flexibility.

A short F is too easily confused with the E.

Very high-waisted. Remember to EXHALE your strokes.

The pen angle must stay quite steep to get these shapes.

The crossbar of H is unusually high. The whole letter is sometimes taller than the other letters in the text.

So plain, but so difficult!

Holding your breath will kill the letters!

1 & 3 are parallel, 2 & 4 are parallel. Overlap at the top. Allow slight concavity

Get the twist in number 1.

Do keep N vertical. The 3rd stroke tends to slope unless done very carefully.

This letter is possible only if you keep a steep pen angle. Be sure to overlap.

Keep the bowl small & droopy.

Look at the inside counter!

Overlap no.1 before forming the tail.

Barely touch the stem before pulling out the beard.

Remember the beard is straight!

S does seem to tilt a bit.

The small top counter makes this letter seem high-waisted too.

Avoid stiffness!

Note the top of the vertical.

This is a V. U is beginning to happen, but hasn't yet. You must also design your own J, R & W.

The top counter is smallest.

The reverse curves of these two strokes make a very graceful letter, but don't overdo it.

Sometimes the Y will be very tall.

Maintain a very steep pen angle.

Note

Speedball C-2

Yvonne Bianco gave me a real assist with this alphabet when she pointed out to me that "tall people write tall, & short people write short." She is much shorter than I, & her juicy black Rustic was indeed much shorter than mine, which was far too stringy & anemic. I like it much better now.

One great advantage of this one is its flexibility. It can be narrow or wide – tall or short, depending on the available space. It can be combined nicely with Italic. (No, not as caps, but as emphasis as a whole word or line' – maybe a title.)

THIS IS A VERSION OF THE MODERN RUSTIC CREATED BY JAMES HAYES. THE BASIC STROKE IS A TWIST FROM ABOUT A 30° PEN ANGLE TO AS NEAR 90° AS POSSIBLE FOR THE VERTICALS. USE A 45° ON CURVES. A FINISHING TOUCH COMBINED WITH A BIT OF PRESSURE SHAPES THE TP OF THE VERTICAL: I'I. A DIAMOND FOOT IS MADE WITH A 30° PEN ANGLE. KEPT SHORT AND DONE FREELY RUSTIC HAS IRRESISTABLE SPARKLE & GAIETY.

As you write this 20th century style (which LJR assures me Mr. Hayes would probably not recognize) remember the insights you gained as you wrote the 5th cen letter. Let the bowls droop a bit & maintain the high-waisted appearance.

Notice that a letter was left out of one word. The correction was put in above.

REJOICE IN HUMANESS!

Machines can't make mistakes. If you compete with a machine on its terms, YOU LOSE! So don't reduce your writing to being like type.

YOU ARE NOT A TYPEWRITER.

Admit mistakes, correct them, & go right on.

Most erasures are a MESS. Simply line through an unwanted letter or word.

The Rustic on this page was written with a Wm Mitchell Rex Pen #3. The Cursive Series is not flexible enough. You want a springy nib which spreads a bit with pressure.

LJR calls this "Square Rustic."

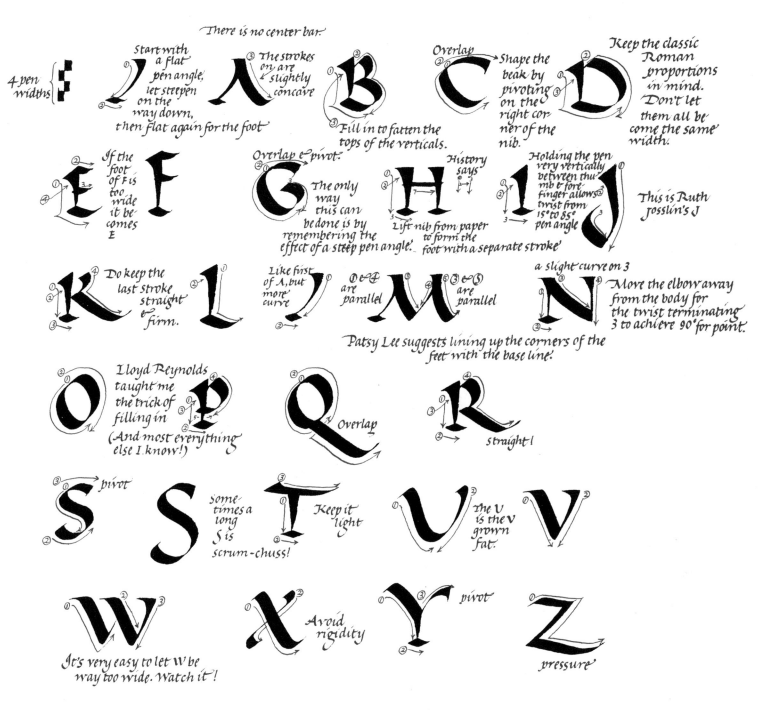

There is no center bar

4 pen widths

Start with a flat pen angle, let steepen on the way down, then flat again for the foot

The strokes on are slightly concave

A

B — Fill in to fatten the tops of the verticals.

Overlap → Shape the beak by pivoting on the right corner of the nib.

C

Keep the classic Roman proportions in mind. Don't let them all become the same width.

D

If the foot of F is too wide it becomes E

E   F

Overlap & pivot. The only way this can be done is by remembering the effect of a steep pen angle.

G

History says — Lift nib from paper to form the foot with a separate stroke

H

Holding the pen very vertically between thumb & forefinger allows twist from 15° to 85° pen angle

I

This is Ruth Josslin's J

Do keep the last stroke straight & firm.

K

Like first of A, but more curve

L

① & ④ are parallel

M ③ & ⑤ are parallel

a slight curve on 3

Move the elbow away from the body for the twist terminating 3 to achieve 90° for point.

N

Patsy Lee suggests lining up the corners of the feet with the base line!

Lloyd Reynolds taught me the trick of filling in (And most everything else I know!)

O

P — Overlap

Q

straight!

R

pivot

S   sometimes a long S is scrum-chuss!

Keep it light

T

U

The U is the V grown fat.

V

It's very easy to let W be way too wide. Watch it!

W

Avoid rigidity

X

pivot

Y   pressure

Z

There is pressure on the thick parts of the strokes. This rules out the use of a rigid nib. Use a fountain pen for personal writing, use a felt nib for demonstrations, but use a flexible nib for these. This page was written with Speedball C-2

Remember that the Uncials are Majuscule letters, although with them we find the Square Caps (MAJUSCULES) beginning to deteriorate; & the lower case (MINUSCULES) beginning to appear.

Time saving devices such as combining strokes & rounding corners change the forms considerably from the slower and even more difficult Romans.

This particular version is discussed briefly in Carl Nordenfalk's beautiful book CELTIC & ANGLO SAXON PAINTING pub. by Braziller. p. 96. He believes it to have been written in the 8th cen. I do find it even more beautiful than the 9th cen. Tours examples. You should look them both up & decide for yourself. There are many different adaptations of Uncial.

THE CODEX AUREUS PROBABLY WRITTEN IN THE EIGHTH CEN TURY PROVIDES AN EXQUISITE MODEL

A speedier version of Uncial appears on the next page, but even it should not be rushed. If you are the "Instant potatoes type" (one used to immediate success who expects to eat ten minutes after hunger is evident:) you must revise your expectations. Calligraphy, JUST AS ANY REAL ART takes a long long time.

An alphabet like this is very slow. Relax & enjoy watching the forms emerge from under the nib. It should not be written or read too rapidly. If you are just supplying information use a different alphabet OR TYPE.

This Uncial is meant to provide, or to assist in providing, an aesthetic experience. HURRY IS ONE OF THE CURSES OF OUR TIME. Slow down. Enjoy what you are doing. Enjoy yourself. Feel the paper under the nib. Exhale with the stroke. Turn away from the tension. Move easy, easy, easy. Lose yourself. Center.

Wm Mitchell Roundhand No. 2

Notice the very flat pen angle throughout.

3½ pen widths

Hairlines are formed by pulling the corner of the nib out of wet ink.

The serifs are drawn with a corner of the nib, & filled in

Think flat on top to avoid

Keep this to the left of this

Another 8th c. example (See Ian Tschichold's TREASUREY OF ALPHABETS, pl. 56a) gives a more careful center stroke & serif. Draw it with the left corner of the nib.

Use the left corner of your nib to draw the top serif & the right corner for the bottom serif.

The center stroke of E & F is as long as the top.

Up on the left corner of the nib & drag.

Draw serifs

It is wide.

This top serif is made by moving the nib parallel to the guide line before making the vertical.

Draw it.

Patience! (who said this was an easy one?)

Very steep pen angle on 1 & 3

Draw the foot.

Maintaining a flat pen angle is tricky. It was probably not so hard with a specially cut nib.

same as F.

Allow the pen angle to steepen to make the little tail on the descender.

Draw the terminations.

Use the corners of your nib.

Use a slightly steeper pen angle for the middle of S

Keep the bowl full!

Draw.

Draw.

Turn to a steep pen angle here if you want this version!

C-2 Speedball

This alphabet is so comfortable and smooth-flowing it is often dreadfully misused. PLEASE REMEMBER THAT IT IS A MAJUSCULE ALPHABET & treat it with the respect due CAPITAL letters. Don't crowd them together. Do keep them vertical. It is very easy to become to casual with the forms. Be serious about them.

In the uncial you see the history of the development of letter forms more easily than in most alphabets. The hand is in such a hurry – so much to do! (Genesis before lunch?) Strokes run together for speed – corners are rounded for ease of movement. Tiny buds of ascenders & descenders begin to appear. By the 7th cen. NATURAL UNCIALS have been developed, extending ascenders until they are as long as the basic body height.

Since this is a Majuscule, you may use Versals if you need to emphasize an initial letter.

WHICHEVER VERSION OF UNCIAL YOU CHOOSE FOR A MODEL, ALWAYS KEEP IN MIND THE FACT THAT IT IS A MAJUSCULE. TRY TO KEEP IT CLEAR, WELL-BALANCED & DIGNIFIED.

The basic characteristics of this uncial are openness & roundness. It is full and generous. Few things in this world are sadder than a stingy, skinny uncial letter.

Use these letters (& all others) appropriately. This Uncial is known as the "early Christian alphabet." It was used for much HOLY work. Please refrain from using it to advertise dry goods or garage sales. A slab serifed Egyptian alphabet would serve those purposes better.

As much as you will enjoy this one resist the urge to become an uncial-freak! Some people have misunderstood so completely they have tried to make uncial serve for everyday handwriting!

Minuscules are very near. Soon half-uncial, & by the 9th cen. we will have Carolingian

A Combing the first 2 strokes changes A & D. then rounding the corner changes D to (+ ? = ᴅ (AVOID ð)

d

e E rounded to one stroke (+ ? = e later losing the join = e

m M to one stroke m, later completely rounded.

n But N hasn't changed much. He waits 400 years.

This page was written with a Wm Mitchell Round hand No. 3½

4 pens high

(Uncial can be done shorter or taller. For many years I did it 5 pens.)

The historically correct ductus was probably but I find it much easier to control when the sequence is reversed. Keep both feet on the same line.

Try for shaping the serifs. Some scribes prefer it. Turn before reaching the line.

Think WIDE!

It will help you stay out of trouble if you keep the top almost flat. Watch the counter. Don't let it become a tomato.

With a small pen it can be done with just 2 strokes. This E is a late one. Keep the middle horizontal above center.

Earlier (4·5c.) E is higher waisted. Top & center are tied together.

Note the clean terminations. It's part of why the letters are so clear. The 4th stroke doesn't rest the line. Just a tiny bud of a descender.

Try G all in one stroke with a small pen.

A slight ascender is important to avoid confusion with a modern n. But remember the letters here are all MAJUSCULES!

NEVER dot this I

You are welcome to invent a more exciting J. The Christians didn't have one.

Either K is o.k. But for both keep the last leg straight. This little hair helps the design. Use it.

The middle must be straight.

Let the slight curve in 2 happen as you relax with the movement. Don't do it on purpose. A tiny turn at the base of 1 creates a bit of a foot. Be sure 3 overlaps 2 down here.

The OUTSIDE of O is round, not the inside counter. So keep your eye the outside as you write it.

Are these counters the same size? They should be!

LJR: "Originally rounded here."

The middle may be left open: R

The counters look the same size unless you turn it up-side-down.

This ½ uncial t is so beautiful LJR used it for uncial. You may find the more historically accurate T easier to space. T is so easily spoiled. Do be careful of it.

stay wide

This U is a bit more formal.

Avoid flipping above the line: V or W

V & W are modern. When your historical model doesn't provide, be consistent with it as you invent.

Keep the descender small.

avoid stiffness.

As is the case with much of the history of the letters, there is disagreement concerning the origin of the half-uncial. Some paleographers feel that half-uncial is the natural next step after uncial, evolving as the hand moves faster allowing strokes to merge & corners to round. In the handsome book DIE ENTWICKLUNG DER LATEINISCHEN SCHRIFT it is stated that the half-uncial is a mixed form based on earlier mixed Roman bookhands & Roman cursive. (The ʒ is very obviously the result of wax tablet cursive, but the τ & N are just as firmly based in the uncial.) I, therefore, feel that the half-uncial shows strong influences from both sources.

The long s, or ſ, may seem strange until you consider the influences of Latin cursive on the formal book-hands. Scratched on wax s was too fragile, so it opened up: ſ, with joins it became f.

No one seriously involved in letters would confuse it with the f. The ſ stops at the base line, while f drops below. f has a cross bar, ſ does not, &, of course, the word helps differentiate.

This page is based on letters written in Tours AD 850. The facimile in 2000 YEARS OF CALLIGRAPHY was my model.

As you write it, please keep the majuscule in mind. Although this alphabet flows much more readily than the uncial, it should still be stately & should remain vertical. Don't fall into the trap of considering it to be a minuscule.

the half uncial aſ written at tourſ in the ninth century iſ ſpaciouſ and heartbreakingly beautiful. the body height iſ only 2 penſ, but the huge ſpace left between lineſ of writing (about 14 penſ) combined with very generouſ counterſ giveſ a very open feeling to the page.

Please be careful to differentiate between half-uncial & Carolingian. To the inexperienced eye they are very similar. The letters which show the most obvious distinctions are a, ʒ, l, n & r. It would be a mistake to substitute the a, g, l, n or r of Caroline.

This page was written with a Wm Mitchell Cursive No. 7 nib.

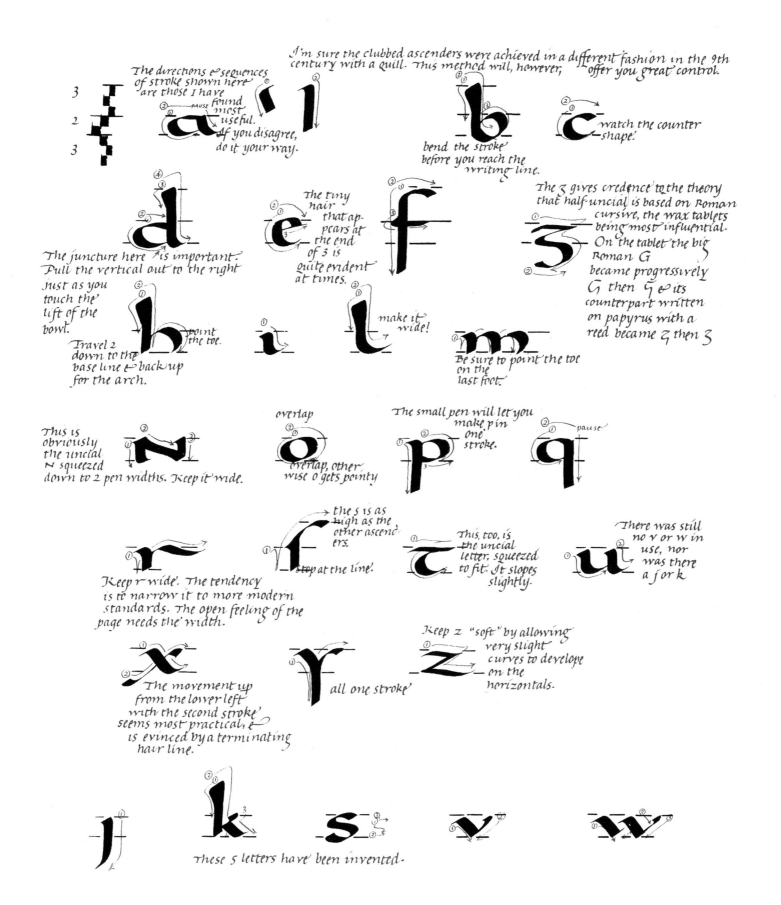

The directions & sequences of stroke shown here are these I have found most useful. If you disagree, do it your way.

I'm sure the clubbed ascenders were achieved in a different fashion in the 9th century with a quill. This method will, however, offer you great control.

bend the stroke before you reach the writing line.

watch the counter shape.

The juncture here is important. Pull the vertical out to the right just as you touch the lift of the bowl.

Travel 2 down to the base line & back up for the arch.

point the toe.

The tiny hair that appears at the end of 3 is quite evident at times.

make it wide!

Be sure to point the toe on the last foot.

The 3 gives credence to the theory that half-uncial is based on Roman cursive, the wax tablets being most influential. On the tablet the big Roman G became progressively G then Ɣ & its counterpart written on papyrus with a reed became Ɣ then 3

This is obviously the uncial N squeezed down to 2 pen widths. Keep it wide.

overlap

overlap, otherwise O gets pointy

The small pen will let you make p in one stroke.

pause

Keep r wide. The tendency is to narrow it to more modern standards. The open feeling of the page needs the width.

the s is as high as the other ascenders.

stop at the line!

This, too, is the uncial letter, squeezed to fit. It slopes slightly.

There was still no v or w in use, nor was there a fork

The movement up from the lower left with the second stroke seems most practical, & is evinced by a terminating hair line.

all one stroke

Keep z "soft" by allowing very slight curves to develope on the horizontals.

These 5 letters have been invented.

Not all Carolingian is sloped. Some is more beautiful than others. I have chosen the fragments from Tours, 850 A.D. as models. There are many examples from which to choose. Tours pleases me most. Realize in choosing your models that not everyone writing was a master scribe, & just because it's old doesn't mean it's excellent. (Of course, that works the other way, too. Just because it's new is no guarantee.) Carolingian is also very beautiful in its vertical form. (See the next page.)

This is the alphabet which Poggio & Niccoli rediscovered in the 15th century, & which became, on the one hand, Humanist Bookhand &, on the other (at least according to some scholars) the Chancery cursive which foreshadows our modern Italic.

I am using the sloped version here to help to demonstrate the possible similarities between it & the Chancery Cursive. Slope is one requisite for the cursive; joins are another. Of course, this lovely, clear letterform is a far cry from the spikey letters which Chancery Cursive became—but they are not unlike the Italic written by such scribes as Bartolomeo Sanvito or Pierantonio Sallandro.

This page was written with a William Mitchell Roundhand nib Number 4. The ruling is 4-2-4, with an extra 8 pen widths to create more interlinear space. This is a very important characteristic of Carolingian.

If you want to save space, use Blackletter!

In the late 8th century Charlemagne sent Alcuin of York to find an alphabet to use as the official alphabet of the holy Roman Empire. These letters had to be beautiful, legible & easily & quickly learned. It had to be rapid to write. (Charlemagne had undertaken an extensive educational program & was anxious to edit the Bible.) Alcuin found an excellent alphabet for such purposes in France where it had superceded Merovingian. It is called Carolingian.

Finally a minuscule has appeared. (It is sometimes called "lower case" because of the old printer's practice of keeping the little letters in a case beneath that which held the majuscules, or "upper case" letters.)

These letters seem almost contemporary to us because we can now recognize all of them except t as lower case. The long s, or ſ may seem unusual, & for modern use must be replaced by the short s.

Uncials, or drawn versals were used as emphasis letters.

Some few, careful joins can be seen. It is not, however, a hurried alphabet.

Smooth, flowing & graceful, it is further enhanced by large interlinear spaces which make for easy passage of the eye from right to left.

Sometimes the ascenders are much more heavily clubbed, but such clubs seem awkward to me, & even ugly. NEVER DO ANYTHING WHICH SEEMS UGLY TO YOU. TRUST IN YOUR OWN SENSE OF THE BEAUTIFUL.

Ascenders are more
than body height

I 2 p.w.

Descenders are
more than body
height.

Let it be wide

a

Keep
the
edges of
the club
serif
rounded

b

The serif was actually formed
but with a large pen
that's hard to do smoothly.
Quills allow
much that
steel
doesn't.

c

d

Be sure the top counter
is smaller than
the bottom one.

e

It seems strange that these letters
should have so many strokes-but those I studied
at the Newberry library DO. Probably part of the effort to control the forms.
They can be done in less, but forms tend to deteriorate.

Interestingly,
I found some
hastily done
f's like
this:
f
which gives
us another
notion of the
ductus of this
letter.

f

The ear of the g is all thats
left of the big
Roman G.
Keep it para-
llel to the
guide lines.
GGg33g
Do use it!
(Although some very distinguished
scribes, among them Sanvito & E. Johnston,
left it off sometimes.) Certainly, NEVER g

g

h

The pointed toe
reminds us of
uncial ancestors.

no jots over ι at this
point in history.

ι

l

m

Except for our
artificially constructed
serif, do it all in one
stroke.

n

o

The 9th cen. scribes DID
use 2 strokes-even though
they wrote very small
letters.

p

start No 3 down
on the base line.

q

pause

r

f

All of my facsimiles show
the exclusive use of the long s with
Carolingian

ſ

τ

u

v

All of these letters can be done in one stroke, but the original fragments I have
been able to examine give evidence of multiple strokes.

x

γ

z

j was not
used until
the 12th cen.
& it wasn't
until the
16th that scribes
began to differentiate
between ι & j.

j

k

It is difficult to squeeze
a good s into 2 pen widths.
Let it drop below the line
if necessary.

s

Beware of too much curve in
v & w.

w

Speedball C-2

You will find many historical pages laid out this way. It demonstrates the interesting phenomenon called the "hiearchy of scripts". Such a page offers the oldest letter forms first. In this the drawn Carolingian Versals (representing antique Roman). They are called "Compound Capitals-Roman style" by Graley Hewitt. Tall, slender & dignified, they suggest the elegance associated with the incised caps.

The second letter is the flat pen uncial which post dates the Roman caps. Then the formal half-uncial, newer yet. Finally, the vertical Carolingian, which was a popular bookhand in the 9th cen.

The decorated versal was simply done in the earlier periods. One can guess rather accurately as to the age of a manuscript by how ornate the versal is. The more ornate the illuminated letter, the later the manuscript.

The term "illuminated" is accurately used only when gold has been used as a part of the color. An illuminated page flashes with light reflecting from the gold on the page. Without gold it is best to refer to the emphasis letter as "decorated."

OFTEN

COMPLETE WORDS were written out in carolingian versals. ut more often they are found being used to emphasize important words & paragraphs.

The Carolingian Versals were filled in, so the forms seem solid. Contemporary artists sometimes leave them open, much to the dismay of more traditional Calligraphers. They are left open on the model page so you can be fully aware of their construction. I like them best drawn & filled in with color. Draw them with the same nib you use for the text. This will help unify your design.

DO CONTEMPORARY DESIGNS! I have arranged this page to show you an historical approach. You should know about it, but don't imitate it! Be a now person. Don't content yourself with emulating the past. Learn the letters so you can use them with unselfconscious ease THEN DO YOUR OWN DESIGNS. Of course its easier to use someone else's layout, but the world of art would indeed be barren if everyone went the easy way. NOR SHOULD YOU HANG ON TO JUST ONE SOLUTION. Move & grow—even though it is sometimes painful.

This page is written with a Rex nib no. 5 & is an example of the vertical Carolingian. In doing it you must be very careful to avoid allowing the letters to tilt backward.

The final figure is a line filler—used to fill out the space in order to create as even a right hand margin as possible. See Edward Johnston's WRITING, LETTERING & ILLUMINATING

These versals were drawn with a Mitchell Roundhand
nib No. 4½. They are 20 pen widths high. Historically there is great variation in size & weight.
You should experiment a bit with them – but – remember – they are a drawn version of the **ROMANS**.

The serifs are done with a
very flat pen
angle.

Leave the tops **bald**.

 Draw the
insides of
the
counters
FIRST.
Then add
the outer
contour.

The serifs
of C are
drawn
with the
edge of
the nib.

You must turn your
nib to a 90° angle to
form the horizontals.
Fill in the serifs by
drawing with
the edge of your nib.

Leave more
space between
strokes at
the top
than at the bottom.

Be careful that the
stems of all the vertical
letters are
wider at
the top
than at
the bottom.

Keeping serifs shorter on the
inside of the letters will
make them
more
beautiful.

Unless you have worked with the written Roman Majuscules
a good deal, it will be very difficult to do these drawn Romans.

Leave it bald!

  Draw &
fill in
serifs.

Do the inside first,
then add the outside lobe.

The corners must be drawn with
the edge of the nib.

No more
than one
pen wide
at the
widest
part.

Let the
tail be firm!

Be sure to grow
the beard from
the chin. R, not R

Think
of X as basically
two straight strokes.

Draw the INSIDES
first.

Remember, the traditional practice was
to fill in all the white space within the
strokes, so the letters look strong.

  L J R recommended that
one line of Carolingian Versals
per page is enough.

Blackletter earns its name by closing up as much of the white space as possible. Legibility is forgone in favor of economy & speed. Gothic, as it is often called, has been popular since the 12th century. German, French and Spanish were among the many scribes to use it, so do not give the old English all the credit, although their beautiful Prescissus is certainly a lovely form of it.

Lloyd Reynolds called this the Christmas alphabet because everyone can read it during the holidays. The rest of the year it is almost illegible. Everyone finds it fascinating because it make such a strong dark area and because it seems so "fancy."

As the student gains experience it becomes apparent to him that more elaborate alphabets are easiest to write. Clear, simple seeming letters such as Roman, humanist, or a good Italic are more difficult and more surely a test of skill with the pen. Letter forms, just as any other art form, are strongest & most beautiful in their early life. They tend to be overflourished and weak as they get older. I like some of the very early 10th & 11th century blackletters to the more rigid 15th century forms such as the one the example on this page is based on. Although attractive, blackletter cannot be considered a good alphabet, because it is usually so difficult to read. After all, the primary function of writing is to be read, NOT TO BE FANCY.

You will find this easy to do, but use it sparingly. Look at modern German work for inspiration.

Close spacing & verticality are major concerns when writing the blackletter. forms vary depending upon period, place & fashion. How ever, they are all upright & very closely fit together, eliminating much white space.

Sometimes the letters were unbelievably small. Much precious space could be saved. Is it any wonder that the scholars were ready for the revival of legible letters by the fifteenth century?

This page was written with Wm Mitchell cursive No. 3 & a clipped crowquill.

This form began to develop as early as the 10th century, as Carolingian was condensed both vertically & horizontally to save space. Generally called GOTHIC BLACK LETTER, it has many sub-classifications. This model is based on TEXTURA QUADRATA, a quite vertical, regularly spaced alphabet, employing a well-defined diamond-shaped foot & triangular top serif. The even spacing between letters is very important & is never more evident than in this letter form.

For this reason I introduce the blackletter to my beginning students. It causes them to become super aware of spacing & that awareness helps improve their other letters.

Other names with which you should become familiar are the TEXTUS PRESCIUSS (the English version.) It's main feature is an absolutely flat foot & a somewhat lighter top serif. It is tall & narrow.

TEXTUS SEMIQUADRATA, an early 12th century form. It has a heavier top serif & a curved foot. It is softer, although narrow.

GOTICA ROTUNDA, the Southern Blackletter, used mostly in Italy & Spain. It is more open, and rounder, using a small top serif & a flat first foot. The terminating foot is usually turned & often understated.

ordinarily short & wide.

When Blackletter was used historically there was great concern to justify the right margin, because an irregular edge would spoil the solid appearance of the text area. Many abbreviations were used to get the right side even.

There are many more variations, but these four are the most influential. FRAKTUR is closely related – but it is a world of its own.

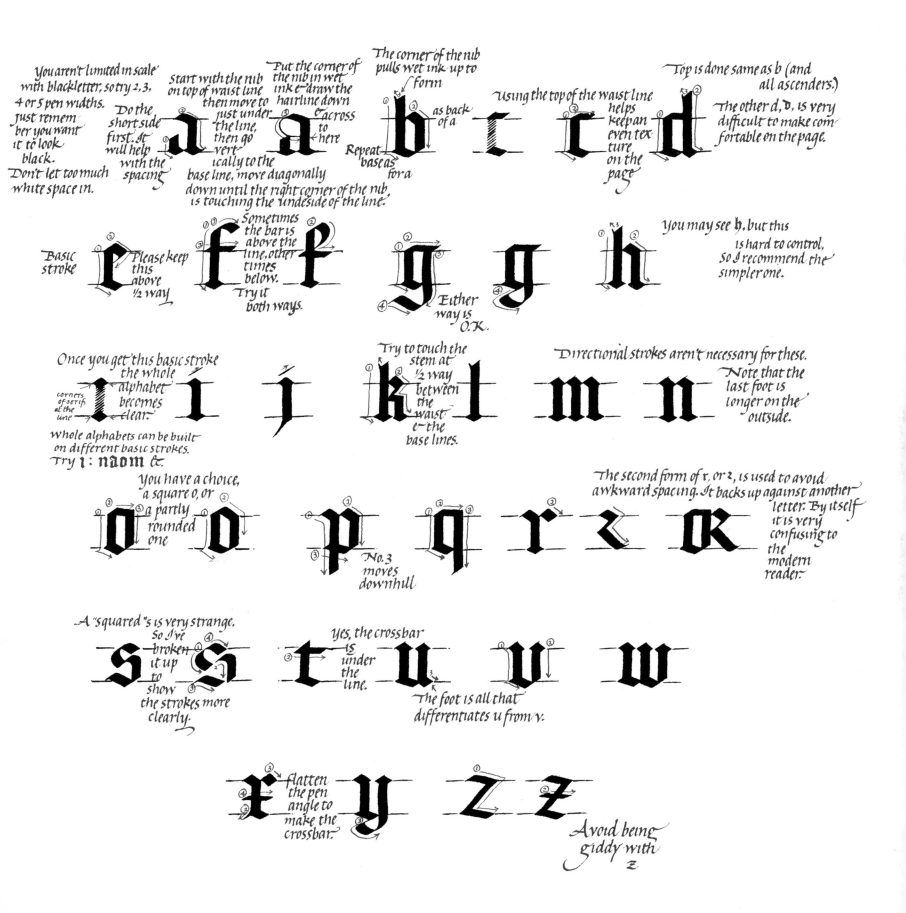

You aren't limited in scale with blackletter, so try 2, 3, 4 or 5 pen widths. Just remember you want it to look black. Don't let too much white space in.

Do the short side first. It will help with the spacing

Start with the nib on top of waist line then move to just under the line, then go vertically to the base line, move diagonally down until the right corner of the nib is touching the underside of the line.

Put the corner of the nib in wet ink & draw the hairline down & across to here

The corner of the nib pulls wet ink up to form

as back of a

Repeat base as for a

Using the top of the waist line helps keep an even texture on the page

Top is done same as b (and all ascenders.)

The other d, ꝺ, is very difficult to make comfortable on the page.

Basic stroke

Please keep this above ½ way

Sometimes the bar is above the line, other times below. Try it both ways.

Either way is O.K.

You may see ♄, but this is hard to control, so I recommend the simpler one.

Once you get this basic stroke the whole alphabet becomes clear.

corners of serif at the line

Whole alphabets can be built on different basic strokes. Try 1: naom &

Try to touch the stem at ½ way between the waist & the base lines.

Directional strokes aren't necessary for these.

Note that the last foot is longer on the outside.

You have a choice, a square o, or a partly rounded one

No. 3 moves downhill

The second form of r, or z, is used to avoid awkward spacing. It backs up against another letter. By itself it is very confusing to the modern reader.

A "squared" s is very strange. So I've broken it up to show the strokes more clearly.

Yes, the crossbar is under the line.

The foot is all that differentiates u from v.

flatten the pen angle to make the crossbar.

Avoid being giddy with z

Although the need for an "upper case" letter was apparent hundreds of years earlier, it wasn't until early Gothic (around the 12 th century) that a majuscule' was altered so that it shared similar characteristics with the minuscule to the extent that they are called the same name.

Until the Gothic period the Roman, written or drawn, or the Uncial served where there was a need for special emphasis. The Gothic- or blackletter- Caps are still basically Uncials, but they are so altered we can think of them only as Gothic. They can no longer function independently. They "go with" or "fit" only with the Gothic minuscules. Although we often see these majuscules used by contemporary designers to form complete words, it is NOT an admirable practise!

LJR: "Paleographers do not think that a true 'duplex' alphabet— one with majuscules & minuscules harmonizing— appeared until the high rennissance."

There are many wonderful versions of these letters. Examine historical & modern texts for others.

The height of the Majuscule depends on the size of the minuscule. I like them SHORTER than ascenders

overlap

A vermilion accent is common.

Turn your nib to 90° for 4

A the little decorative elements have been made with the same nib used to write the letters.

② is done by pulling wet ink out of ① with the corner of the nib.

The ticks are made by maintaining the pen angle & moving left to right. Like the rest of this alphabet it LOOKS harder than it is!

DOWNHILL

It is generally a good idea to make horizontals lighter than verticals.

Fill big white counters to avoid holes on otherwise "black pages."

Please opt for the simpler versions of Gothic

C-2 Speedball

The decoration here was done with a pointed crowquill. Tiny fine spotting brushes are good to use. For color I use an opaque tempra, but the possibilities for color are greatly varied.

Egg tempra was much used in the middle ages.

To learn to lay gold is another very special art. The Guild of Scribes & Illuminators is the most elite guild in the world. Ruth Josslin is becoming our West Coast expert, & I am indebted to her for her help in illuminating.

Notice the ligatures. There are many more than I can show here. It is permissable to invent your own, as long as they are convincing.

The scribe in the scriptorium was seldom the rubricator (who added the red) or the illuminator (who added the gold) or the miniaturist (who painted the tiny illustrations"). Usually the main text was written out by the scribe. He would leave empty spaces – with sometimes a tiny indication of what was to fill in the space so the other artists would know what to put there.

Of course the important books done for rich clients (such as the Duke Du Berry) were much more elaborate than simple school texts.

Sometimes a book would not be completed – perhaps a client died – or was dissatisfied with the project. At any rate, the decorations were done AFTER the Calligraphy. This is still a good practice.

Draw the outlines of your Versal with the same pen you have used for the text. You may draw the outline with the same color you use to fill in the heavier areas. I don't care for black outlines.

The passage of time tends to make art form more elaborate. So, by the fifteenth century a considerable change had taken place in the versal letters.

The small area above was written with a Mitchell #7.

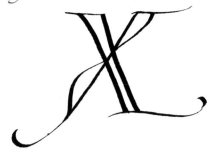

Let them be free! Overworking & correcting spoils their spontaneity. Rigor mortis is undesirable in anything!

Please do the more formal Carolingian Versals first. These Lombardic Versals are a later form, based on Uncials, but the same basics apply.

Let the top be wider than the bottom.

Draw the INSIDES first.

don't let the lobe be wider than the widest part of the stem.

The strokes across the ends of the stems & extruders are always curved as though part of a huge circle!

Be sure the tops & bottoms of the rounded parts are BALD.

Don't let the lobes creep too far. NO!

NO!

It is considered best practice to fill in the letters to a solid color. Use them as Versals, i.e as INITIALS.

The model given here is my version of Lloyd Reynolds' version. Mr. Reynolds has made the 16th cen. form much more legible, & therefore useful, than it would otherwise be. The brief paragraph at the bottom of this page gives you something of an idea of how very difficult the "real" thing is. For a quite detailed study of the script, I suggest Samuel A. Tannenbaum's book THE HANDWRITING OF THE RENAISSANCE, pub. by Frederick Ungar, N.Y.

You might enjoy writing this alphabet in color: It is amazing how different it seems when written in pale blue or Spring-time green. Of course it is its most powerful in plain black with perhaps a vermilion accent.

The rhythm is very different from that of Italic, even though they are both cursive alphabets & share a sloped appearance as well as joins.

This page was written with a Wm Mitchell Roundhand Nib #3.

There seem to have been as many versions of this alphabet as there were persons writing it. Some of the more consistent forms were named. In the 12th cen. the Gothic script was divided into two main categories: THE COURT HAND which was quite free & hurried and THE TEXT HAND which was much more formal, slowly written & precise. By the late 14th century a wide variety had been developed, all of which were called Bastard Script, meaning a compromise between formal & informal. Most secretaries wrote several versions. Early in the 15th century "a small Court hand" developed which in the 16th cen. became the English Secretary hand. It was used combined with "the sweet Roman hand"— or Italic. Often the text of a letter would be written in the Secretary hand & signed in Italic.

This is a modern version of a 16th century cursive Blackletter called Bastard. (A name which covers many variations.) In England it is called Secretary & tends to be more vertical.

The drooping termination of the h is a definite characteristic of this alphabet.

The e is a double stroke, eliminating the top counter: ι + ~ = ℮, causing confusion with c which is shorter: ι + ~ = c, & with t which is taller: ι + ~ = t. (There were also other forms of e.)

The several kinds of s: ſ, ſ & ſſ would be most obscure to modern readers.

Shakespeare wrote a secretary hand. None of his holographs exist but we have his signatures.

v.r

v.r

The pen stayed on the paper as much as possible, sacrificing legibility to speed.

It's great fun to play with, but use it sparingly, IF AT ALL!

Watch the inside counter! Shaping the white circle is the only way to get the hang of it.

The first stroke looks like a bird

Be sure to slope the letters for this version.

l c o i a b c

The counters are not round inside b & d, but try to have them the same size.

d e f o g

turn the nib to a steeper angle

leave the top open

Let the second foot drop below the line!

h i j k l m

n o p q r s

simply ride the pen angle down.

It (s) can go below the base line.

both are done in one stroke.

t u v w x y z

L.J.N. prefers 'X²'

Try to have the Majuscules *shorter* than the minuscule ascenders. SLOPE.

Don't try to get clear into the stem with no. 2.

you may want to break the curve here as with O, i.e. C

I A B C D E

Keep horizontals LIGHTER than verticals.

F G H I K

Turn the nib to 90° angle for these.

L M N O P

Be careful that the cross of T moves downhill to the right.

Q R S T U

V W X Y Z

The need to clarify handwriting was first acknowledged in the 9th cen. when Charlemagne wanted to solidify the Holy Roman Empire, & rightly decided a common hand would help. It was then that Alcuin found, modified & put to use the beautiful Carolingian. As time went by and more & more had to be recorded on less & less space on smaller & smaller skins the Carolingian deteriorated into Blackletter. By the time of the Humanist Revival in the 15th cen. paper had become common enough to allow more generous use of writing material, so when Caroline was rediscovered by the 15th century scribes it was possible to use its modified version. This alphabet could not have survived without the generous space provided by ample surface.

You will find this alphabet to be the workhorse of your repertory of letters for formal work. It is comfortable & inconspicuous. (Sometimes you don't want the letters to demand attention.) Because early type fonts were based on these forms, they are familiar, & therefore easily learned. When the main purpose of a letter form becomes to convey information as clearly & simply as possible, then the alphabet should "stay out of the way." The Humanist Bookhand does just that.

Although this ANTICA TONDA is quickly and easily read, it is not as quickly & easily written as the blackletter. This is an alphabet for the EYE. LJR likened the history of the letters to a battle between the hand & the eye. The hand moves faster & faster, dropping parts, rounding corners & tying forms together, until the eye can barley discern the parts. Then about every 500 years someone says "WHOA! I can't read what you have written!" At such times scholars, searching through history (usually for some other reason) find an alphabet to revitalize, modernize & put to use. So far the alphabet has been basically the same one each time. CAROLINGIAN.

What a relief to the eyes Humanist Bookhand must have been when it joined the beautiful but illegible Blackletters in the late 14th century. It is credited to three scholars: Coluccio Salutati, Poggio Bracciolini & Niccolo Niccoli* for recovering the literary treasures of ancient Rome and with them Carolingian *lettera antica* - the old letter. It served as a model for the Humanist scribes. By the middle of the 15th century printing had begun to replace the scribes. Humanist Bookhand was used as a model for type, so it is very familiar to us today.

Of course, Carolingian was very attractive to the Humanist scholars for many reasons such as its legibility, its simplicity - which made it easy to learn - & its handsome appearance. Most important to them was its ANTIQUITY. They believed it to be antique Roman, because so much early Roman literature & history had been recopied in Charlemagne's time in Carolingian. Actually, the ancient Romans had no minuscule letters. The closest they came to it was Latin cursive.

Found first in the 9th. century by Alcuin, next by Francesco Petrarca in the 14th century (his hand is called FERE HUMANISTICA or Near Humanistic) & then again (after the fiasco of copperplate and pointed steel nibs) by Edward Johnston in England in the 20th century. Who will discover it again 500 years from now? Under what circumstances?

* Their work was done in the 15th cen.

A 30° pen angle.

3½

4½

3

This first letter is apt to have an unwanted hair line, but I like it anyway.

For work you want to reproduce this one is better.

This is an artificial way to make a serif, but it works with a large nib.

Start the branching stroke way back in the stem to avoid a hair line here

Form the serif by pivotting your nib to a steeper angle as you complete the second stroke.

With a small, flexible nib, try forming the serif by initiating the vertical stroke with SLIGHT pressure: l

Try for the same amount of white space in d as in b, p & q

The center of e sits on a line ½ way between the top & bottom

pivot like c under the line

Line up

slight foot

The ear is at the side & under the line

A small circle over an OVAL

A jot over i is seldom necessary.

Keep inside foot short

But j needs one. Keep jots from cluttering precious interlinear space.

The counters of m are narrower than the counter of n.

Avoid hair lines by branching high & starting the branching stroke in the vertical

At least 2 pen widths inside n's counter

Overlap to avoid hair lines

THINK ROUND

k 90°

Keep the grin off his face (p<)

The ear of r must stay short - or spacing is a problem.

pivot

Watch the counters while you make s. They should LOOK the same size.

pivot

The counters are Roman archs.

Cross below the line

Think of a u for the base of t.

Notice this counter.

The second side doesn't go above the line.

Two STRAIGHT STROKES!

Notice stroke 4

Only entrance curves! Keep the rest of the strokes straight.

Same here, but add exits.

Try to keep it from tilting.

A slight reverse curve.

SLIGHT curves

Once you get control of this alphabet you earn the right to experiment as on the next page.

C-2 Speedball

How mind boggling it is to realize that all the letterforms with which we are familiar in the western world have evolved from the Roman Majuscules. As the hand hurries faster & faster corners get rounded & strokes get combined. Different writing materials also effect the the shapes. The wax tablets were very influential in their contribution to the deterioration of the Classical Romans. But human ingenuity and inventive imagination must receive due credit for many of the developments. Purposefully manipulating the basic elements of the letters is a worthwhile exercise for any calligrapher. It becomes almost a responsibility to move beyond the models ONCE YOU TRULY UNDERSTAND THEM. Slavish copywork is not desirable, nor is groundless "self expression." To experiment try changing scale, slope, height, width, relationships between body height & ascenders and descenders, serifs, speed of writing, tools, surfaces, writing fluids, rhythm & whatever else occurs to you (I just remembered PEN ANGLE!) Some of your results you will hate, but some will be quite attractive. Keep an open mind, & return to your model for a refresher now & then.

When you vary the basic characteristics of a letterform, separately or in combinations, the changes can make a significant difference in appearance. All the alphabets on this page are variations of Humanist Bookhand.

2 pen widths
& a simple
serif

abcdefghijklmnop
qrstuvwxyz

Whatever changes you make, be consistent throughout.

Try a little pressure when you initiate the vertical stroke. Then release the pressure to form the serif.

abcdefghijklm no

A little pressure here

pqrstuvwxyz

Changes of pen angle make dramatic differences. Notice changes in counter shapes.

abcdefghijklmno
pqrstuvwxyz

Make the letters wider. Try making the basic serif smaller.

abcdefghijklm
nopqrstuuvvwx
yz

These letters represent only a few of the changes possible.
Before experimenting you should understand Humanist Bookhand.

The Roman Majuscules are the most perfect, & by far the most difficult. Because of their magnificent design they are amazingly flexible. They may be done 10 or 12 pens high - as were the Inscriptional Romans - and the result is tall elegance. Strong & yet graceful, such letters - well done - require years of study. They may be done as short as 3 pens high - as in the written Square caps. Solid & black, they are yet flowing & alive. And they may be done in a proportion pleasant to fit with Humanist minuscules. Here I have chosen to make them 7 pens, in order to go well with the version of Humanist Bookhand presented in this revised edition of WRITTEN LETTERS. Since it is necessary to have majuscules with a minuscule alphabet, & since no other letters will fit as caps for Humanist bookhand, the student must learn to do them well enough without a model. Remember, we are ALL still trying to do the Romans. They are an ideal which we will never really achieve. It is no shame to find them difficult. Anyone who thinks they are easy is probably doing them wrong.

You will seldom have to write out whole words using this version of the Caps. When you do, however, pay special attention to the spacing. Even a slight variation in the spacing will be uncomfortable. Crowding them is particularly painful!

Mitchell Roundhand Nib no. 3

FOR CAPS WITH BOOKHAND

Memorize the various letter widths. One huge disservice type has done has been to equalize the widths of the upper case letters. In type an E is often as wide as an M. Remember, in any art form, the eye is delighted with variety

No doubt, if they had been easy, none of the other letter forms would have developed. All the alphabets we have in the Western world have evolved from the Roman Majuscules. SO WE MUST BEGIN - AND CONTINUE BEGINNING.

Fill in the brackets.

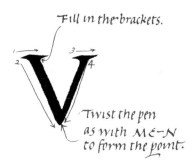

Twist the pen as with M & N to form the point.

2 & 5 are parallel
4 & 7 are parallel

The bottom counter is slightly larger than the top.

Slightly below ½ way

All one stroke. You must manipulate the pen angle to maintain weight to the line.

No Roman should look weak

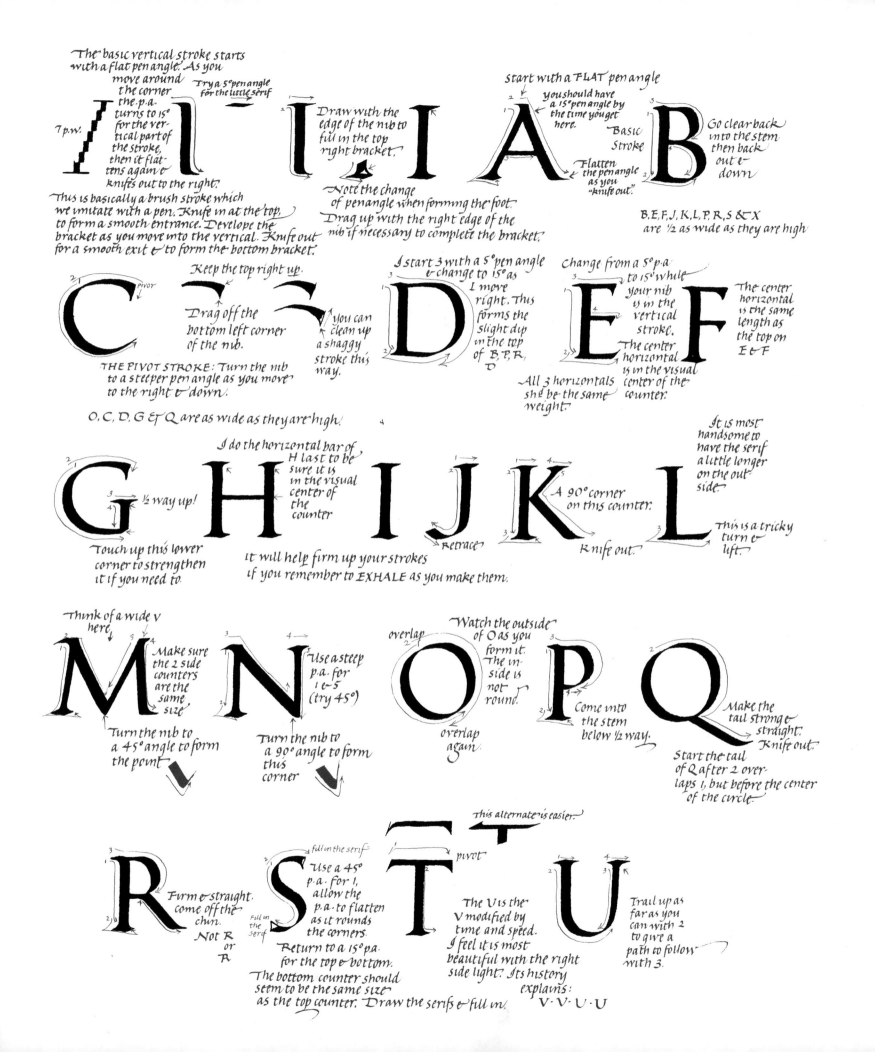

The basic vertical stroke starts with a flat pen angle. As you move around the corner the p.a. turns to 15° for the vertical part of the stroke, then it flattens again & knifes out to the right.

1 p.w.

Try a 5° pen angle for the little serif

This is basically a brush stroke which we imitate with a pen. Knife in at the top, to form a smooth entrance. Develope the bracket as you move into the vertical. Knife out for a smooth exit & to form the bottom bracket.

Draw with the edge of the nib to fill in the top right bracket.

Note the change of pen angle when forming the foot.

Drag up with the right edge of the nib if necessary to complete the bracket.

start with a FLAT pen angle

you should have a 15° pen angle by the time you get here.

Basic Stroke

Go clear back into the stem then back out & down

Flatten the pen angle as you "knife out."

B, E, F, J, K, L, P, R, S & X are ½ as wide as they are high

Keep the top right up.

pivot

Drag off the bottom left corner of the nib.

THE PIVOT STROKE: Turn the nib to a steeper pen angle as you move to the right & down.

You can clean up a shaggy stroke this way.

I start 3 with a 5° pen angle & change to 15° as I move right. This forms the slight dip in the top of B, P, R, D

All 3 horizontals shd be the same weight.

Change from a 5° p.a. to 15° while your nib is in the vertical stroke.

The center horizontal is in the visual center of the counter.

The center horizontal is the same length as the top on E & F

O, C, D, G & Q are as wide as they are high.

½ way up!

Touch up this lower corner to strengthen it if you need to.

I do the horizontal bar of H last to be sure it is in the visual center of the counter

it will help firm up your strokes if you remember to EXHALE as you make them.

A 90° corner on this counter.

Retrace

Knife out.

It is most handsome to have the serif a little longer on the outside.

This is a tricky turn & lift.

Think of a wide V here

Make sure the 2 side counters are the same size

Turn the nib to a 45° angle to form the point

Use a steep p.a. for 1 & 5 (try 45°)

Turn the nib to a 90° angle to form this corner

overlap

Watch the outside of O as you form it. The inside is not round.

overlap again.

Come into the stem below ½ way.

Make the tail strong & straight. Knife out.

Start the tail of Q after 2 overlaps 1, but before the center of the circle.

this alternate is easier.

fill in the serif

pivot

Firm & straight. come off the chin.

Not R or R

Fill in the serif

Use a 45° p.a. for 1, allow the p.a. to flatten as it rounds the corners. Return to a 15° p.a. for the top & bottom. The bottom counter should seem to be the same size as the top counter. Draw the serifs & fill in.

The V is the V modified by time and speed. I feel it is most beautiful with the right side light. Its history explains: V·V·U·U

Trail up as far as you can with 2 to give a path to follow with 3.

How often we are asked to make posters for well-meaning, but misunderstanding friends! Twenty signs for the school carnival by Monday ··· labels for the PTA bazaar ··· Somehow the lovely historically oriented letter forms seem uncomfortable & out of place for such events. This funny little alphabet (try it in color) seems just right for many of those occassions.

Because, as Carl Dair says in his most useful book, DESIGN WITH TYPE, there are only TWO kinds of letter structure—many ways to shape them, but only 2 structures: ① shaded line letters & ② monoline letters, it is important to know about monoline. For these examples, I have used the Speedball B-series nibs. With considerable manipulation you can do monoline with a chisel nib, but it is, at best, a very awkward endeavor. C.D. says, & I agree, that knowing this form will enrich your design capabilities by making the contrast of structure available to you. He further suggests consideration

This can be a useful variation.

You recognize these slab serif letters (called Egyptian by some calligraphers) as being those used on many typewriters. But realize it would be a mistake to try to make your work look as if it were done by a machine. Let your letters change size, let them bounce & turn. A machine is limited to a straight line, YOU AREN'T!

The idea of two letters being exactly the same is based on type. "Human beings were not meant to work with the accuracy of tools." (John Ruskin THE NATURE OF GOTHIC – if you can find a copy, read it.)

So purposely vary your letters–yet keep them somewhat consistent. This may be more of a challenge than it first seems.

This example was done with a Speedball B-4 nib.

of such contrasts as: 1. SIZE: Using different nib sizes can be an effective source of design. Use a strong contrast or it may seem that you inadvertently picked up the wrong pen.

2. COLOR: One touch of color can bring a page to life. If you are using only one touch, be very careful of its placement! Familiarize yourself with the Golden Section.

When you are doing something personal, there is no rule saying you must limit yourself to any particular color combination. Just be aware that when working for unknown persons, they will be more universally pleased with black, white & vermilion — even though you, personally prefer something else.

The most usually successful color combination is BLACK (the ink) WHITE (the paper) & VERMILION. (I find Shiva Nu-Tempra tube color most useful – but not a bad vermilion can be mixed of Prang pan water colors.) To make these paints more durable mix in a bit of water base glue, such as Elmers. Thin with water & fill your nib with a brush rather than dipping.

3. WEIGHT: Letters made of thin lines are called "light"; those made of fat lines are called "heavy". LIGHT - **HEAVY**.

4. DIRECTION: Your brain is so wonderful it can read words backwards or upside down. So words need not always be horizontally oriented. Consider contrasting horizontal with vertical. But DO NOT STACK. not HOTELROOM / HOTELROOM
Instead, turn them.

Be very careful with the diagonal. It is most powerful & requires considerable design experience. Avoid stairsteps.

5. TEXTURE: As well as the texture of stroke, i.e. a rough line as those done with a reed or a smooth line as one done with a quill or a steel pen, you should be aware of the areas of texture created by a mass of letters on a page – as if cloth.

6. SHAPE: This contrast is necessary if we have letters at all. Each letter has its own shape. The more contrast between the letters, the easier the words will be to read. An alphabet made up of too similar shapes is not usually useful.

Whenever you use a new tool, familiarize yourself with it first. Play with circles & straight lines. The B-series nibs are not round. Learn to manipulate to achieve a consistent monoline.

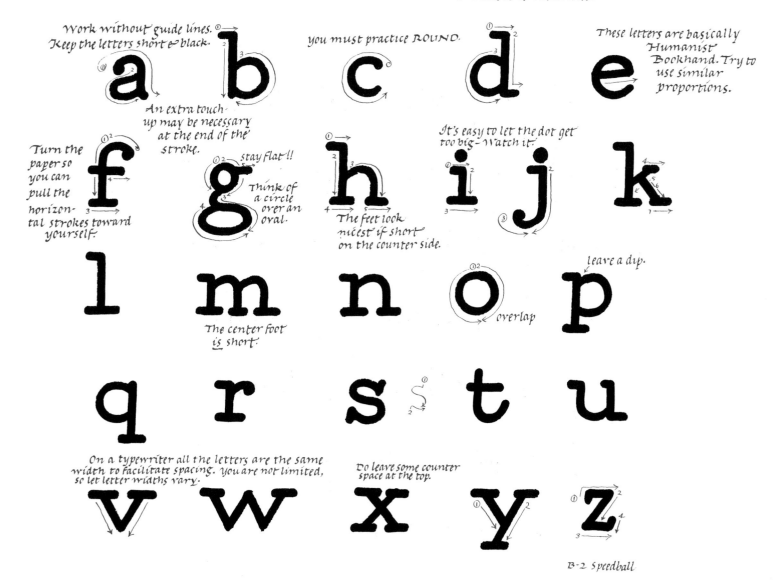

Work without guide lines. ⓪→
Keep the letters short & black.

you must practice ROUND.

These letters are basically Humanist Bookhand. Try to use similar proportions.

An extra touch up may be necessary at the end of the stroke.

Turn the paper so you can pull the horizontal strokes toward yourself.

stay flat !!

Think of a circle over an oval.

It's easy to let the dot get too big — Watch it.

The feet look nicest if short on the counter side.

The center foot is short.

leave a dip.

overlap

On a typewriter all the letters are the same width to facilitate spacing. You are not limited, so let letter widths vary.

Do leave some counter space at the top.

B-2 Speedball

Never do anything ugly! The letters on this page please me, but — unaltered from the type — they would seem ugly to me.

These upper case letters were done with a B-5 nib. They are really quite different than those on your typewriter — because I could not bear to write the ugly forms on my machine. So I have redesigned the caps for you.

These letters will fit with the lower case (which is also changed) & yet recognize the source — ROMAN.

Perhaps you choose to overlook this style. O.K.!

(But you should know about it.)

A B C D E F G H I J
K L M N O P Q R S T
U V W X Y Z

What a beautiful thing it would be if all type-designers were first calligraphers. Such training would assure that most type faces would be well-designed—with concern for the history & understanding of the development of the letter forms.

We have so easily given up so much beauty in our lives & our world because ugliness seemed to be more "financially expedient." How often is a poorly trained person hired for a job rather than a well-trained person who wd "cost more." What false economy!

Those type faces designed by persons of taste as well as training are very handsome as well as useful. It takes experience to recognize them. Rest assured that just

Many lettering artists spend their time carefully drawing outlines of letters & then filling them in with a brush. Their models are usually mechanical type faces. The main reason for this procedure is to allow more freedom in spacing than mechanical type can allow. Type precludes overlaps. Each letter must be a certain measured distance from the next letter. The artist can draw the letters so that the counters within words are more pleasingly designed.

To be able to draw letters is a valuable, saleable skill. It is much easier to draw the forms if you know how to write with a flat-edged pen. Many typefaces are closely related to the pen.

Ernst Schneidler designed the typeface Legend. It would be foolish to try to duplicate type with a pen. Allow the letter forms to change as the pen dictates.

because a type exists does not mean it is well designed. Your responsibility when using type goes well beyond simply pointing to an example in a book. There are many good teachers & books available to you concerning type. But choose carefully! There are many persons to whom Calligraphy seems a fad! - & an offshoot of "legitimate" letter forms. Lack of study clouds their perspective. Type is such a RECENT development in the history of letter forms!

Of course, if you don't control the pen you will lose the form entirely - but don't force it!

All of the strokes on this page are simple and require only moderate manipulation - less manipulation by far than the Roman Majuscules.

This page was written with Wm Mitchell Round hand nib 3.

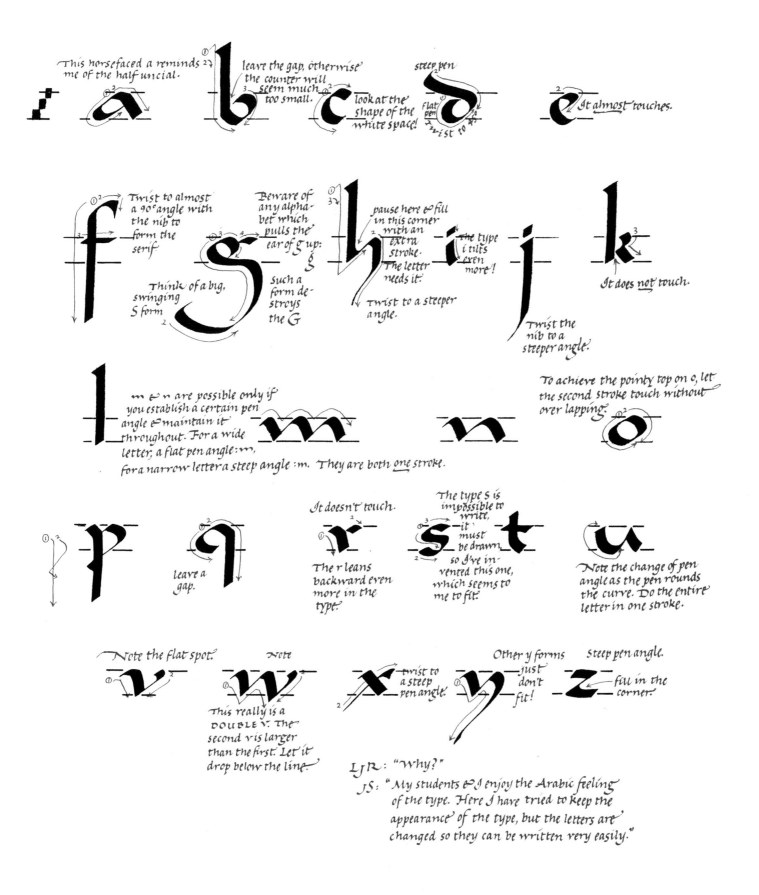

This horsefaced a reminds me of the half uncial.

leave the gap, otherwise the counter will seem much too small.

look at the shape of the white space!

steep pen

flat pen twist to

It almost touches.

Twist to almost a 90° angle with the nib to form the serif

Think of a big, swinging S form

Beware of any alphabet which pulls the ear of g up:

Such a form destroys the G

pause here & fill in this corner with an extra stroke. The letter needs it.

Twist to a steeper angle.

The type i tilts even more!

Twist the nib to a steeper angle.

It does not touch.

m & n are possible only if you establish a certain pen angle & maintain it throughout. For a wide letter, a flat pen angle: m, for a narrow letter a steep angle: m. They are both one stroke.

To achieve the pointy top on o, let the second stroke touch without over lapping.

leave a gap.

It doesn't touch.

The r leans backward even more in the type.

The type s is impossible to write, it must be drawn, so I've invented this one, which seems to me to fit.

Note the change of pen angle as the pen rounds the curve. Do the entire letter in one stroke.

Note the flat spot.

Note

This really is a DOUBLE V. The second v is larger than the first. Let it drop below the line.

twist to a steep pen angle.

Other y forms just don't fit!

steep pen angle.

fill in the corner.

LJR: "Why?"

JS: "My students & I enjoy the Arabic feeling of the type. Here I have tried to keep the appearance of the type, but the letters are changed so they can be written very easily."

Some persons will doubtless be dismayed to find
such typelike letters in a Calligraphy workbook.
To them I must explain : Some kinds of letters
do one job, others another. It is, I believe, a mistake to believe that any one letter form or style
can possibly do all the work required of letters.
It would be inappropriate to write a note to
the milkman in Uncial, & equally dismay-
ing to advertise a boxing match in Italic.
A truly well-rounded Calligrapher should
be aware of the vast world of type & its
tremendous potential. Very few of the
fonts are adaptable to written, Calligraphic
purposes. Legend, Egyptian & Neuland are
among those which can be adapted to a pen.

Be sure the lower case ascenders are taller than the upper case letters.
(The term "lower case" came about because in print shops the minuscule letters were stored in a case beneath the majuscules, which were, likewise, called "upper case.")

START DOWN HERE

Note pen angle changes from a flat to a steep angle as the letter progresses. It can all be done in one stroke!

The same shift from flat to steep pen angle as on B.

Twist to a steep angle.

Of course you can leave the top knot off, but it's much less like Legend.

L looks so much like a one stroke letter with a stylus it can be!

wow!

Fill up the "valley" with an extra stroke

If you change them too much they won't be Legend.

Another wow!

Note the pen angle changes.

Broaden the ends of this stroke by drawing.

Thicken by double stroking.

All one stroke. Go back & fill in the bottom of the counter.

fill in

I've modified these letters as much as seems possible so they can be written with a pen, & yet retain the "flavor" of the type.

To write Ernst Schneidler's

Legend so that it retains its

Near Eastern appearance and

is yet free of the restrictions

of type presents a new set of

problems.

These letters are very different
than the typeface Legend.
They are based on some forms
Schneidler wrote as he
was developing the typeface.
They are written
very
rapidly.

Mitchell Roundhand 3½

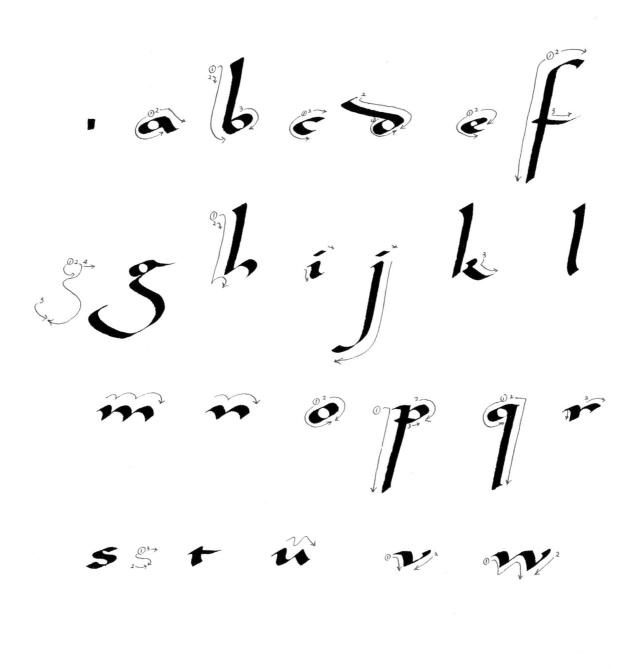

At this point it might prove useful to consider some
of the "formal" and "informal" aspects of the letters.
Just as the word implies, some letters are formal, i.e.:
carefully & slowly written with considerable concern
for perfect, copybook forms. Some very formal practice
suggests that each part of the letter be made with a
separate stroke. Such form would avoid any push
strokes, & would be limited to movements from top
to bottom and from left to right. The resulting
letters tend to be quite stiff, but appropriate to some
situations. Informal writing will employ as few
strokes as possible. The graceful, rhythmic development of the word & the text area is of greater concern than the perfection of each individual letter.
Very informal writing becomes personal script
which uses frequent joins to facilitate speed. To me,
Italic seems the only alphabet suitable for such very
informal use. It remains legible despite joins and
speed.

*Revised for more rapid writing & to be used
with the less formal minuscules on page 38
these majuscules have the same stroke sequences
as those on page 34.*

A B C D

E F G H I

J K L M

N O P Q R

S T U V

W X Y Z

When you travel, be sure to go to Germany. Some of the most exciting contemporary work with letters is being done there.

Strictly speaking, much of the work being done in Germany cannot be called calligraphy (which is beautiful writing) because many of the letters are not written. Rudolph Koch drew, wove, cut & carved Neuland. At the beautiful Klingspor Museum in Offenbach, Germany, you will see some of his amazing wall hangings. The letters he used varied with the material used. When he changed letter size, he changed letter shape. Both were adapted to fit the media. A brush written Neuland varies from a woven Neuland, which is still different from a pen-drawn or wood-carved Neuland. Yet, each time he used it, it was unmistakably Neuland. Short, dark, &-as he used it-closely packed. The only white space between verticals in Koch's work is the almond-shaped sliver left by the curve of the letter. Of course, the end result is difficult to read, but very dramatic-as is usually the case with blackletter. Whole areas of texture become very important-more important than the separate words.

Neuland can be used less dramatically by involving more white space. It is immediately more legible-as is any alphabet-when more white space is evident.

THE NEULAND IS DESIGNED TO BE PACKED

Forming these letters with a chisel nib requires considerable skill. LJR says Koch originally designed the Neuland printing type by cutting directly in the metal. This explains why the letters are so un-pen-like — therefore requiring considerable manipulation. Koch did draw them with a pen. You will see examples at Klingspor.

In order to draw this alphabet with a chisel nib you must forget 2 rules of written work: ① do not retrace strokes &. ② do maintain a consistent pen angle – because these letters are double-stroked & the pen angle changes often.

A consistent pen angle is a most useful thing! In many alphabets once you have learned the pen angle the letters almost shape themselves. When you do not have such an aid it becomes necessary to be particularly aware of line widths in order to achieve consistent weight. Learning this alphabet is therefore a very valid experience.

Try it as a wood-block letter where shaded line (thick & thin) letters will not do – the thin being so fragile. Also, cut it out of black or colored paper with a razor blade or Exacto knife. Glue it in place with rubber cement. Used this way it's a natural for quick, effective bulletin boards & public labels.

This example of Neuland was drawn with a Speedball C-2 nib.

This page was also done with a Speedball C-2 nib. The letters are taller than those on the opposite page — so you can see the counter spaces more easily.

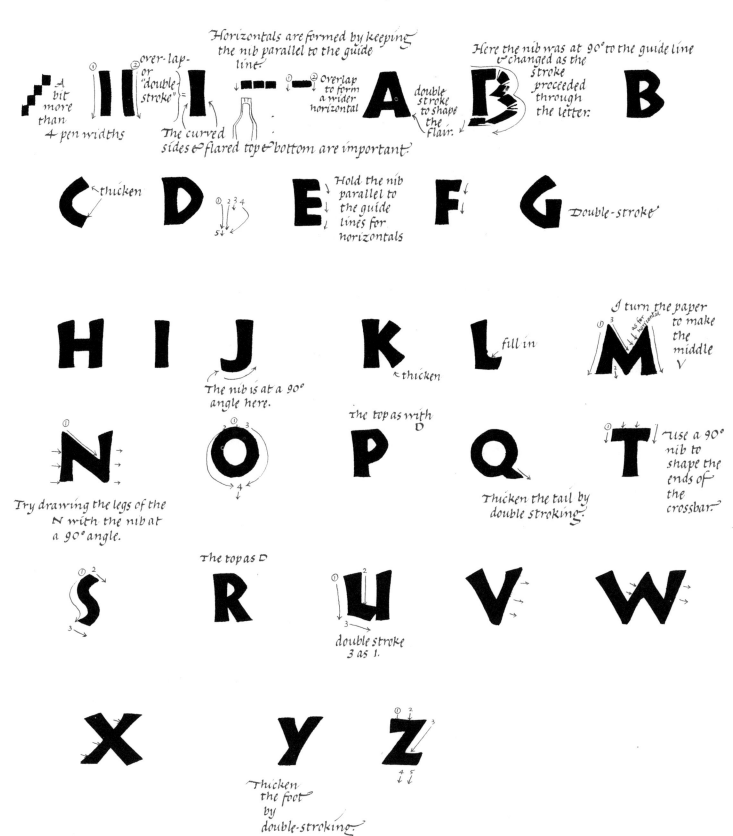

A bit more than 4 pen widths

① over-lap ② or "double stroke" =

The curved sides & flared top & bottom are important.

Horizontals are formed by keeping the nib parallel to the guide line.

① ② Overlap to form a wider horizontal

double stroke to shape the flair.

Here the nib was at 90° to the guide line & changed as the stroke proceeded through the letter.

thicken

① 2 3 4 ⑤

Hold the nib parallel to the guide lines for horizontals

Double-stroke

fill in

thicken

I turn the paper to make the middle V

① 3 as for horizontal ②

The nib is at a 90° angle here.

Try drawing the legs of the N with the nib at a 90° angle.

The top as with D

Thicken the tail by double stroking.

Use a 90° nib to shape the ends of the crossbar.

The top as D

double stroke 3 as 1.

① 2 3 4 5

Thicken the foot by double-stroking.

Read EDWARD JOHNSTON, a biography written by his talented daughter, Priscilla Johnston. Not only will you find the book charming to read, you will come away well informed about this remarkable man to whom the calligraphic revival owes such an immense debt. Ms. Johnston also gives us considerable insight into the beginnings of the calligraphic movement in England in the late 19th & early 20th cen.

E. J. was introduced by W. R. Lethaby to a long-time friend of the great William Morris,

Everyone involved with Calligraphy must have, & use WRITING & ILLUMINATING & LETTERING, written by E. J., and first published in 1906. It is chock-full of useful information & Calligraphic wisdom. Here I quote his statement on the qualities of good lettering: "The first general virtue of lettering is readableness, the 2nd, fitness for a given use. & the rational basis of the following summary is the assumption that such fitness is comprised in beauty & character; & that a given piece of lettering having readableness, beauty, & character has the essential virtues of good lettering. # The qualities on which these virtues seem chiefly to depend, & their special significations in the case of plain writing seem to be may be set forth as follows:—

Long a basic alphabet taught in England, Mr. Johnston's foundational hand is strong and black & delightfully variable.

Sir Sydney Cockerell. Cockerell was aware of beautiful writing & illuminating due to Morris's interest in it. Cockerell drew E. J.'s attention to the 10th cen. Winchester Psalter (Harley MS 2904) which influenced him so greatly in the development of his Foundational Hand. (It shd be noted that the 10 c. Psalter is a late Carolingian, tending toward Blackletter. E. J. loved to pack it & make it dark, thus enhancing it with the juicey seductivity one finds in the Blackletters rather than the rather Spartan spareness of some of the 15th cen Humanist Bookhands.)

It was Lethaby who arranged for E. J. to teach the first modern-day Calligraphy class at the Central School in Upper Regent Street in London in Sept., 1899. There were seven students in the class.

READABLENESS. 1. Simplicity: As having no unnecessary parts. (and being simply arranged.) 2. Distinctiveness: As having the distinguishing characteristics of each letter strongly marked. (& the words distinctly arranged.) 3. Proportion: As having no part of a letter wrongly exaggerated or dwarfed. (& as the lettering being proportionally arranged). BEAUTY. 4. Beauty of form: As having beautiful shapes & constructions, so that each letter is an individual & living whole … fitted for the position… 5. Beauty of uniformity: As the assimilation of the corresponding parts… & as the "family likeness" of the letters… 6. Beauty of the arrangement: As having a general fitness in the placing, connecting & spacing of letters, words, & lines, in the disposal of the lettering in the given space; & in the proportioning of every part of the lettering & its margins. CHARACTER. 7. Essential qualities of (Hand & Pen) work: As being genuine Calligraphy, the direct outcome of rightly made & rightly handled pen. 8. Freedom: As having skilled & unaffected boldness. 9. Personality: As having the characteristics which distinguish one person's hand from another."

Thus example is 3½ p.w.

Sometimes my stroke sequence is different than A.C.'s or M.A. Even E.J. changed at times. You should try other ways, too.

Start no.3 here

spring from within the stem to avoid forming a hairline.

Be sure to overlap 1 with 2

drag

No hairline should appear where 1 & 4 come together.

e does seem to lean backward a bit.

Give it a strong foot.

E.J. did leave the ear off the S "when in Rome..."

spring strongly.

give a good indication of feet. The outer foot is strongest.

Notice that the guide lines are penetrated. If you want to remain within lines rule 4 p.w.

No hairline

start here with 2, so the branching is strong.

Make positive overlaps to avoid hair lines.

The inside counter is not round. Rather, the outside of 1 & the inside of 2 form a circle & the inside of 1 & the outside of 2 form a circle.

E.J. leaves this lovely little counter.

crop the ear when the word requires it for spacing sake.

At the end of a word it can fly!

s is quite sturdy... not too narrow.

It really works quite well to do the cross bar first when you aren't joining it to the following letter.

It is interesting to find different serifs, but try making them the same, & see the difference.

Try to keep the last of w from swinging up above the waist line. W←NO! V←No!

Be sure this overlap is strong, so 3 doesn't seem just "tacked on."

Thank you Ieuan Reese, Donald Jackson & Peter Thornton all for helping me understand these beautiful British letters a little better.

Ann Camp in her very helpful book PEN LETTERING & Marie Angel in her lovely new book THE ART OF CALLIGRAPHY both offer excellent, concise models for slightly different versions of Edward Johnston's letters. One of the wonderful things that has happened in the past ten years has been the big increase in the number of books available to us for study

IT IS BEST TO SIMPLIFY THE CAPS IF YOU PLAN TO WRITE OUT WHOLE WORDS WITH THEM

These majuscules were written with a William Mitchell Round-hand nib No. 3½. I've been told that the Wm. Mitchell pen factory has been acquired by new owners who plan to once again produce fine pens for us by upgrading the old pen making equipment. Therefore I have used Mitchell Round-hand nibs for all

of the letterforms. Responding to increasing interest all over the world, calligraphers & teachers of calligraphy are producing many volumes that can help us all. As a student it is your business to learn from them all with an open, enquiring mind. Calligraphy is the "dance of the pen," & a great dancer knows many steps. There is no ONE WAY to dance, & no ONE WAY to write. We must learn dancing & writing by doing as much of both as we can.

the "text" pages I've done for this revised book.

Another nice thing is happening to help this Calligraphic Renaissance along. Groups of letter lovers are forming all over the country. People are getting together to help & encourage one another. Many classes are being formed. Check at your nearest college. Some people have found one another by advertising in their local paper.

LjR used to say in order to become a Calligrapher one should study Modern Dance, drawing, poetry & learn to play the Violin.

These letters are based on examples of E. Johnston's writing reproduced in FORMAL PENMANSHIP. Hopefully some of the spirit remains in them. His examples are not tight & dogmatic.

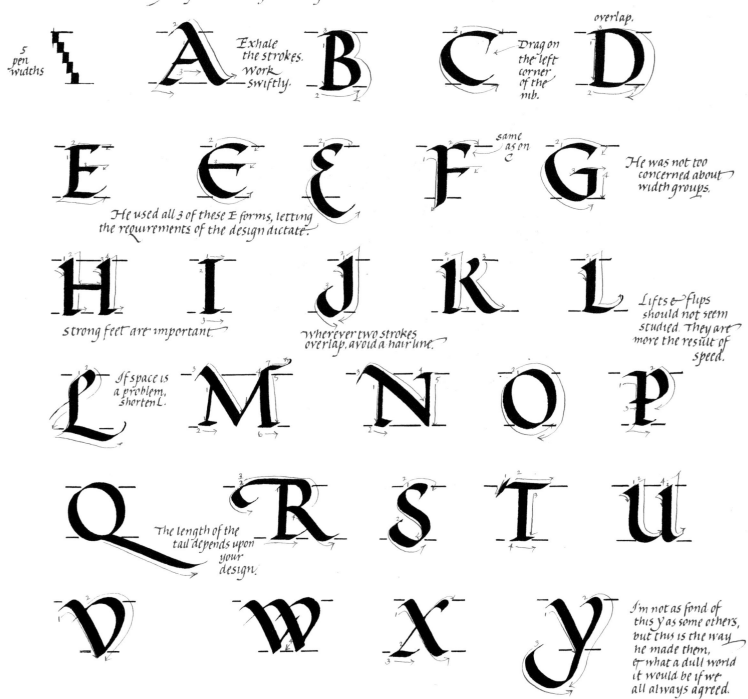

5 pen widths

A — Exhale the strokes. Work swiftly.

B

C — Drag on the left corner of the nib.

D — overlap.

E E E — He used all 3 of these E forms, letting the requirements of the design dictate.

F — same as on C

G — He was not too concerned about width groups.

H I J K L — Lifts & flips should not seem studied. They are more the result of speed.

strong feet are important.

wherever two strokes overlap, avoid a hair line.

L — If space is a problem, shorten L.

M N O P

Q R S T U — The length of the tail depends upon your design.

V W X Y — I'm not as fond of this Y as some others, but this is the way he made them, & what a dull world it would be if we all always agreed.

Z

c-2 Speedball

This little Bone alphabet was developed in about 1972. I invented it as one of many tricks I used to encourage my students to loosen their fingers & wrists. Almost all of the historical alphabets require some manipulation of the pen angle at one point or another. Stiff, inflexible grips on the pen preclude the relaxed, graceful movements necessary for REAL calligraphy to happen. So we've tried many devices to try to help the student overcome the rigid wrist problem.

Working with color helps. Somehow black on white seems very formal - requiring our BEST EFFORTS - which, unfortunately, in our culture implies a lot of up-tight tension. Tension kills the calligraphic dance. Y'gotta let go! Get the swing. Find the beat. We thin down transparent watercolor or opaque gouache & feed it to our pens with a brush. A few minute's practice will help you find the proper consistency.

Try writing without guidelines. (Once you know the letters. Use them until you do.) Arnold Bank - what a wonderful man - & great calligrapher - once told me: "Writing with guide lines is like trying to dance in a broom closet!"

Using home-made pens will help. Make them from yardsticks & tongue depressors, popsickle sticks & reeds, cardboard, stimudent toothpicks.... the list goes on & on. A sharp knife can transform a stick into a pen : ⟍⟋ cut off the top to form a crisp edge. Soak it in ink or paint & write. Bone was originally done with chopsticks which come with a ready-made bevel.

Calligraphic drawing requires much the same kind of pen manipulation as the Bone alphabet; but I find many of my students even more insecure about their drawing skills than their writing skills. DO SOME DRAWING! It will help your calligraphy.

Arthur Baker's skills at pen manipulation can be admired in several of his books published by Dover. While looking at them, however, keep in mind Mr. Baker is a very well-rounded, skilled calligrapher whose talents certainly are not limited to this sort of pen play.

frame
the white spaces with the black lines

Many people "doing" Bone are missing on very important aspect of it: the interletter spaces. When packed snugly together these wiggley letters create some great shapes between them. If the letters are kept too far apart the shapes between aren't allowed to form. So, pack them together. Let them touch one another. Lloyd called this "the most sensuous alphabet of all."

It is fun to do - but use it mostly as a learning device. Certainly, it must not replace any other alphabet, only enhance them.

You should know Humanist Bookhand before you do Bone.

This page was done with a ½" pen made by Philip Bouwsma, & a Wm Mitchell Roundhand no. 3.

Bone can be tall & thin or short & fat. Consistency is desirable.

Try using a dry nib to trace uncovering one line at a time to feel the twist.

It's called Bone because of the bonelike shape of the vertical stroke.

The basic stroke starts with a flat pen angle·goes steep in the middle & then flattens out again. you must roll the pen holder between your thumb & forefinger & twist your wrist.

A little more than 3 p.w.

a twist

It will help if you see the counter shapes

The bottom of the vertical twists *more* than flat.

You may want to invent new letters once you get the hang of the basics. The second e "happened" just this last year while I was demonstrating for students. Stay open for miracles!

not so much twist in this vertical. It just doesn't work

It's just Book hand with a new twist.

Sometimes you will have to dot the i

I like it open on top.

Note the flat feet. They give stability.

look at the counter shape.

Many varieties are possible. When you start making words you will want to vary forms to make attractive patterns.

Drag on the corner of the nib for the hair line

Remember; it helps to exhale the strokes!

Flatten the p.a. in here

You may touch up rough spots with the corner of your nib.

These are among my favorite v's & w's. They just work so well!

Be sure 2 overlaps 1 or this letter seems to fall apart.

Enjoy these letters! Relax & play. They are meant to be an educational TOY. (If you come up with some great new forms, please send me a copy!)

OSTEON SEEMS TO BE A GOOD NAME FOR BONE CAPS

The philosophy behind the Majuscules is the same
as that behind the Minuscules. Play to find out what
your pen can do — what your fingers, hand & wrist
can do. Let your imagination loose. What you learn
playing with these letters can help you put life into
your REAL letters.

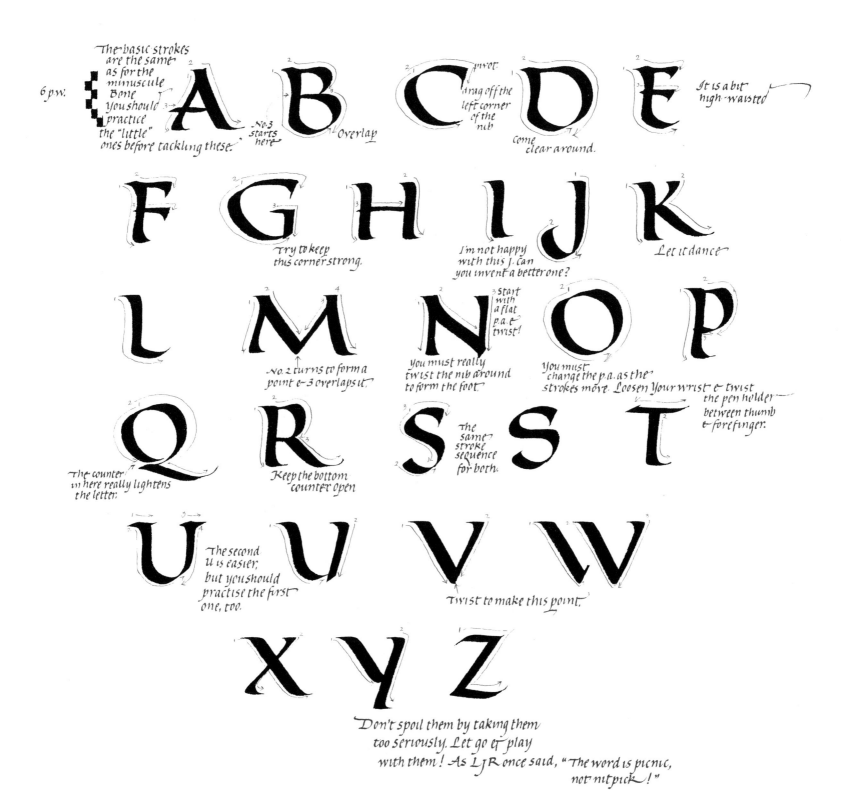

The basic strokes are the same as for the minuscule Bone You should practice the "little" ones before tackling these.

6 p.w.

No. 3 starts here

Overlap

pivot. drag off the left corner of the nib

come clear around.

It is a bit high-waisted

Try to keep this corner strong.

I'm not happy with this J. Can you invent a better one?

Let it dance

Start with a flat p.a. & twist!

No. 2 turns to form a point & 3 overlaps it.

you must really twist the nib around to form the foot.

You must change the p.a. as the strokes move. Loosen your wrist & twist the pen holder between thumb & forefinger.

The counter in here really lightens the letter.

Keep the bottom counter open

The same stroke sequence for both.

The second U is easier, but you should practise the first one, too.

Twist to make this point.

Don't spoil them by taking them too seriously. Let go & play with them! As LJR once said, "The word is picnic, not nitpick!"

These letters were done with a soft, old, worn out C-2

This is the one alphabet we should all have in common. It is the one which can be successfully used as an everyday hand, rapid enough to be used ALL THE TIME. Written with a pencil or ball point pen it remains legible; even under the stress of speed. When the writer can slow down enough to develop a rhythmic flow & maintain a 45° pen angle with the edged pen, the italic becomes very beautiful as well. Any one really serious about becoming a Calligrapher will use a personal version of a calligraphic hand for all ordinary daily writing. Italic seems best suited for the job. As long as you cling to that ugly commercial cursive they thrust upon you in Elementary School you are just kidding yourself. (How can teachers' Colleges possibly continue to ignore the history of something as vital as handwriting? They continue to ignore the advice of experts & use materials & forms which have proven unsatisfactory.) For a long time good books to help with the teaching of italic cursive in the elementary schools were not available; & there was an excuse not to recognize the italic. Now, however, good manuals are to be had. (I recommend most particularly, the ITALIC HANDWRITING SERIES by Barbara Getty & Inga Dubay. The BEACON WRITING BOOKS by Alfred Fairbank are unexcelled, but would be, perhaps, more difficult for the average teacher to use in the classroom.)

Italic: the fine Italian hand, sometimes called the sweet Roman. The experts do not agree on its origins. Some say it is the fraternal twin of Humanist Bookhand, compressed & sloped by speed. Others believe it to be the Blackletter Secretary clarified by association with rediscovered Carolingian. No matter what its past, it is enjoying a great 20th cen. revival as the one calligraphic alphabet which can become a rapid, every day, cursive handwriting.

It is very unusual to find someone writing rhythmically under formal circumstances unless he writes an informal italic. Your personal rhythm comes through after you have learned the alphabet well enough to move quickly with it. Once you establish your own rhythm, it seems to stay with you, even when you slow way down for very formal work. FORMAL is defined as being unjoined and more closely related to the best model. VERY FORMAL letters are broken into as many strokes as there are parts to the letter: i.e: the letter n would be made ı+ı = n. In such practice the letters are stiff &, maybe, more perfect. My models for Italic are semiformal. The little red writing is informal. It has some joins, but it is not as fast as my daily handwriting.

It seems, to me, to be a mistake to use joins when writing with a large nib. Joining is characteristic of personal handwriting & is therefore more typical of, & appropriate to small writing.

If you would like to be better informed about Italic & its modern revival, join the Western American Society for Italic Handwriting, c/o Reed College, Portland, OR., in America, or The Italic Handwriting Society, c/o Fiona Sturdy, 69 Arlington Road, London, NW1.

Wm Mitchell R.H. No. 4

Guide lines for ascenders & descenders should
be thought of as lines beyond which you will not go
rather than goals you must reach.

5

A 45° pen angle is essential for this version. (which is the only one which can easily become handwriting.)

Maintain a good arch.

Keep the ear of r up unless it bumps another letter.

5 p.w.

ɩ + ɩ n m u r r

45°

If you make a vertical cross with a 45° p.a. both strokes will be the same weight.

Italic slopes between 5° & 12° to the right. 5° is best.

Begin the branching at ½ way. Achieve it ⅔ of the way up.

2 or 2 & ½ p.w. in the n counter

Keep the 2 sides parallel. u is n up-side-down

1½ p.w in the m counter

Keep the 2 sides parallel. u is n up-side-down

Then it may droop slightly.

5

n all in one stroke

m

u

Note this counter

v

Exhale on the way down. (It will eliminate the wobbles.)

All in one stroke. The same width as the n.

Historically, i wasn't dotted until the blackletter made it necessary. I use a dot only when there would be confusion without it.

You may use either one, but don't use them both on the same page.

pierce the guide line

The pen angle flattens on the way around. stays flat for this stroke

just under the line. Use about a 15° p.a. to cross f & t.

Start t with the nib ½ a width below the waist line—then move up on a 45° angle line until the left corner of the nib sits on the line. No.2 tucks into the resulting triangle.

l h i j k f t

l

h

i

j

k

f

t

The basic shape of a is so important because six letters depend on it. So study it carefully.

pierce the guide lines.

a very narrow bottom

d has 2 strokes o + l = d

Benardino Cataneo uses g as q. These days it makes a fine g. You must study Cataneo.

I love this alternate Q. But use it sparingly.

Keep the 2 sides parallel

o a d g g q Q b p

maintain this counter

g is much more graceful when done all in one stroke rather than 2. Keep plenty of ink & a light touch.

you must flatten the pen angle for the tail.

flat base

2 strokes

o

a

o+l

g

g

q

G²

b

l+2

This is an ellipse ½ as wide as it is high.

overlap!

Become familiar with the counter!

overlap

overlap

When writing rapidly it is permissable to distort the middle of e with a join: en. But when working formally, maintain the horizontal middle.

Keep strong, open arches on s, even if you must drop below the guide line to do so.

Flatten p.a. to strengthen the mid-part of z.

o c e s z

o

c

e

s

z

Don't go above the waist line.

Think of 4 straight lines. The very slight curve comes later.

Maintain the pen angle on 2 to get the necessary weight.

Do the old 2 stroke y first, because the newer y is an attempt to write y in one stroke. You will be learning them both. Until you can do y, you can't even see y, much less write it. y seems easier because you are doing it wrong.

Avoid v or u with tails.

v w x y y y y

this stroke is incomplete so you can see how it was made. Bend at the line.

It should be completed this way.

not too stringy here

It doesn't get clear down to the line.

v

w

x

y

y

LJR: "Down steep, over wide."

The Italic Capitals are the Roman Majuscules sloped & flourished. The same proportions should apply to both. It has been only in the 20th century revival of Italic that the caps have begun to slope like the minuscules. When Ludovico degli Arrighi prepared his famous & delightful OPERINA, the first writing book on Italic, in 1522, he flourished his majuscules mightily, but they remained upright...closer to the antique Roman.[5]

Please remember when using the Operina as a model that to flourish the caps so much seems very old-fashioned. Such embellishments work well only in the hands of a MASTER like Arrighi, & usually are miserable failures when attempted by anyone else. So very often novices rush into wild flourishes long before they have learned the basic letter forms. A strong flourish only weakens an already weak letter. A good rule of thumb concerning flourishes: Use flourishes only when they enhance a word or its meaning. When the flourish overwhelms the word IT IS TOO STRONG. Also, bear in mind that the Operina was reproduced by wood-carving. The letters were cut on a plank the actual size of the book. This carving led to some spikiness which one does not find in Arrighi's direct writing. ie: n instead of n, & m instead of m. In the wood carved letters the lifts tend to be sharper, too: ie: a instead of a. Refer to plate 32 in Fairbank's A BOOK OF SCRIPTS. to compare a photograph of Arrighi's direct writing with the pages in the Operina. It seems a shame to allow spikes on your italic because you don't understand the problem.

DO NOT WRITE OUT WHOLE WORDS WITH FLOURISHED ITALIC MAJUSCULES. SLOPE THE ROMAN A BIT IF YOU WANT AN ITALIC-LOOKING CAPITAL WORD.

How many times we have all seen the hopeless jumble resulting from an entire word-& sometimes even whole lines of words-being written out in flourished Italic Majuscules! Such examples should prove to you that everything in print is NOT a valid model. Use your best judgement before imitating any of them. Remember, there is no excuse for confusing the reader with displays of virtuosity.

It has always been the downfall of any art form when the artists become bored with good form & so let their work get "fancy." You can date many manuscripts by the development of the decorations... the fancier the later.

Don't contribute to the downfall of Italic by being tempted into showing off!

Can you imagine writing backwards just to prove...what...? Giovanbattista Palatino did it in 1561 when he tried to outdo Arrighi. See the LIBRO NUOVO.

This page of SLOPED ROMAN was written with a Rex pen no. 4

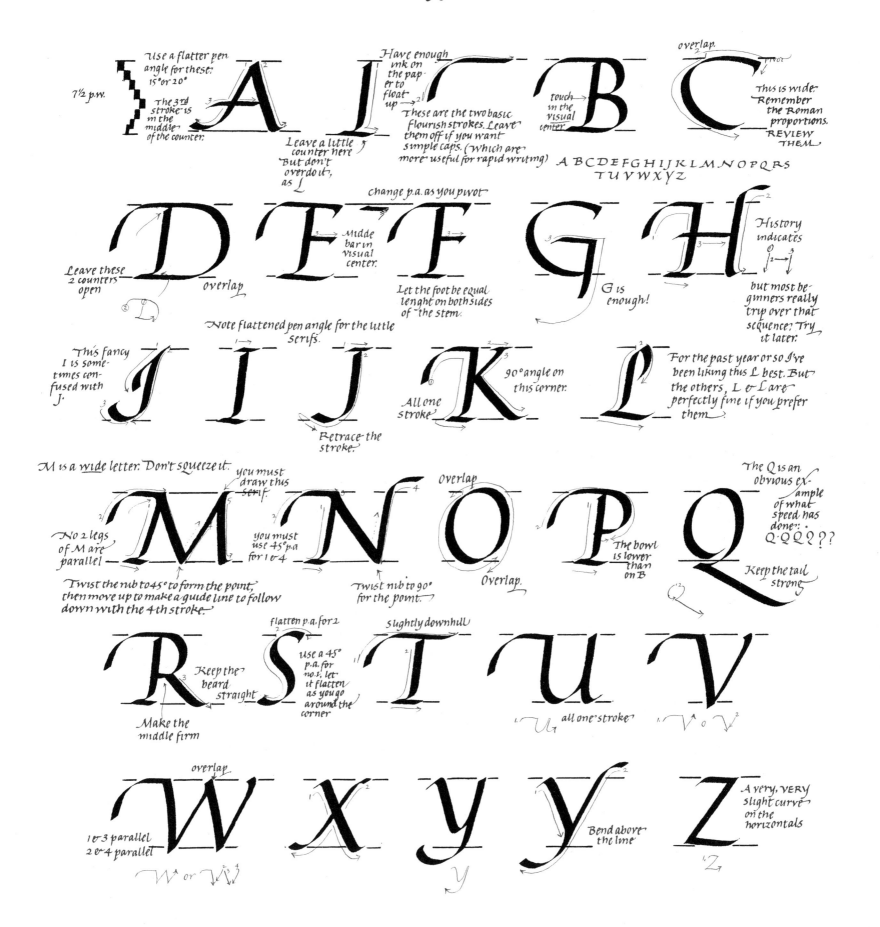

7½ p.w.

Use a flatter pen angle for these: 15° or 20°

The 3rd stroke is in the middle of the counter.

Leave a little counter here But don't overdo it, as

Have enough ink on the paper to float up

These are the two basic flourish strokes. Leave them off if you want simple caps. (Which are more useful for rapid writing)

touch in the visual center

overlap

nor

This is wide. Remember the Roman proportions. REVIEW THEM.

A B C D E F G H I J K L M N O P Q R S T U V W X Y Z

Leave these 2 counters open

change p.a. as you pivot

Overlap

Middle bar in visual center

Let the foot be equal lenght on both sides of the stem.

G is enough!

History indicates

but most beginners really trip over that sequence. Try it later.

This fancy I is sometimes confused with J.

Note flattened pen angle for the little serifs.

Retrace the stroke.

All one stroke

90° angle on this corner.

For the past year or so I've been liking this L best. But the others, L & L are perfectly fine if you prefer them

M is a wide letter. Don't squeeze it.

No 2 legs of M are parallel

you must draw this serif.

you must use 45° p.a. for 1 & 4

Overlap

Twist nib to 90° for the point.

Overlap

The Q is an obvious example of what speed has done: Q·QQ??

The bowl is lower than on B

Keep the tail strong

Twist the nib to 45° to form the point, then move up to make a guide line to follow down with the 4th stroke.

Keep the beard straight

Make the middle firm

flatten p.a. for 2

Use a 45° p.a. for no.1, let it flatten as you go around the corner

slightly downhill

all one stroke

W 1 & 3 parallel 2 & 4 parallel

overlap

Bend above the line

A very, VERY slight curve on the horizontals

The renaissance of beautiful writing in the Pacific Northwest is due, for the most part, to Lloyd Reynold's interest in italic handwriting. He was convinced that the frustrations most students experience with ugly, illegible handwriting contribute greatly to the problems they have in school. Those of us who have had the opportunity to introduce italic to young children have found their delight in making beautiful letters & producing handsome pages does, indeed, influence the pleasure they have in doing school work. The advantages to good spelling are obvious. No longer can mistakes be hidden in accident prone letters. The e and the i remain unlike even when written very rapidly with a ball point pen or a pencil. Because of good joining habits a & o will no longer be confused. The elliptical shoulder maintained on n, m, h will eliminate similarities to u, li, w or v. Realizing that loops are not necessary & that loops contribute to making letters ugly & illegible will help a great deal.

For those of us interested in more artistic uses of the letters, the all-important rhythmic aspects of your more formal work will be greatly enhanced if you will learn & use italic for your daily handwriting. Why italic? Because, written with a 45° pen (or "edge") angle, italic allows the letters to be joined, or "tied" together, thus enhancing speed. This makes it possible to write fast enough for every day use. Safe joins must be used, however, in order to prevent the deterioration of the forms.

To begin your handwriting practice, understand that what we are doing is <u>hand</u> writing. The movements originate in the calligrapher's HAND, not the fingers or the arm. Your wrist must be flexible to allow the hand to move comfortably. A rigid wrist forces the writing into the fingers or arm. Finger "writing" is really drawing & requires great skill. Arm writing is not practical for daily work with a small nib. Both finger & arm writing movements easily deteriorate into spikey forms. Spikes, however, are not natural to hand & wrist movements. Spikey writing is undesirable because it contributes to illegibility. When spikes occur the necessary elliptical shoulder disappears into pointy confusion:

This is the elliptical shoulder Undesirable spikes

n m h   n m h   v w u li

n & m turn into v & w. The h becomes li.

By maintaining the arches we eliminate one of the major causes of illegibity. Practice the elliptical arch by making the arcade: mm mm mm mm. This simple HAND movement is also the basis of the very important rhythmic movement which will bring your writing to life & make it <u>yours</u>. The rhythm is based on DOWN, UP; DOWN, UP. The down movement feels more friction, the up movement glides so lightly the pen almost leaves the paper. Sometimes it actually does as you make diagonal joins:

The diagonal join

nun nun nun nun (try it—over & over—LIGHT UP, FRICTION DOWN) It will help you maintain the 45° pen angle if you will continually move your paper to keep your writing just in front of yourself rather than allowing your writing hand to move to your right. The diagonal join (thank you, Alfred Fairbank) will also help you maintain the 45° pen angle. When the join is 45° & the pen angle is at 45° the resulting line is the thinnest mark your pen can make. That fact, coupled with your light upstroke will make the join so thin it disappears.

More, now, about joins. The number one rule: NEVER MAKE A JOIN IF THE RESULT IS HARD TO READ. Legibility is a prime requsit of handwriting. Usually we are safe joining into or out of a letter which holds a hand out. The n is a perfect example. It has a "hand" out on both sides, so we can join into it or out from it most of the time:

A "hand" → nine nun men mane none answer

However you must beware, because there are some letters it is best NOT to join into or out of even if the friendly n is next to them. Join into an a form; a, d, g, q only from a horizontal:

fan tan vain rain waist

Sometimes letters BUMP - but it isn't really a join.

Joining into the a forms from the diagonal will inevitably lead to their collapse. Used with normal writing speed the diagonal join will pull the a open, i.e. nu, or cause loops, i.e. na.

We also avoid joining into ascenders or out of descenders. Such joins create the loops which distort the letters & create confusion. Copperplate engraving with a burin created loops, imposing them upon italic forms. Hidden inside every ugly, loopy commercial-cursive letter is a cursive italic form:

b b d d f f g g h h j j k k l l p p q q
t t y y z z

All you need to do is lift your pen ever-so-slightly from the surface of the paper so the loops happen in the air rather than on the paper & you will find those hidden letters.

You will use three times as many e s as any other letter, so it must remain very clear. Making e in TWO STROKES AT ALL TIMES is essential. Yes, I know you can make a one stroke letter look the same, but it will collapse into the accident-prone loop e if you join into & out of it. The loop e closes up too easily: ι ι ? then what is it? This enigma: w is one of our major legibility problems. Join into the 2 stroke e this way:

mi me no men money

Let the middle of e become diagonal when you join from it. Otherwise it is horizontal.

①mi   ②me   no overlap

Maintain a diagonal join from e : e. Avoid en & en.

Join into the elliptical o the same way: mo . A two-stroke o allows a neat exit : mom. But be careful ! om, om look awful. Lloyd didn't join from o. Alfred used a horizontal exit join which seems too heavy when done with an edged pen. It's o.k. done monoline.

Join from the crossbar of f & t :

fits fester fortune toffee

Remember to shape s nicely when you join it : asp, not asp. Use joins only when joining. It's silly to write e or s. When you lift your hand to reposition your paper, joins may be omitted, but do join as much as possible for rhythm & speed.

You can write italic cursive all the time. A flat-edged pen & extra care will make the letters more beautiful, but they will remain legible with ordinary tools & more rapid pace.

Try using a ball point pen, a pencil, or, as Arnold Bank suggests, "a stick in the sand."

Several good books are available to help you with your daily handwriting. Some of them are listed at the back of the book.*

* Look for Numbers 13, 15 & 42 in the Bibliography.

Italic handwriting doesn't all look alike!
Personal touch & rhythmic movement makes
every hand distinctive.

Here are a few clips
from some of the
hundreds of
beautiful letters
sent to me, just
to demonstrate
some variations.

Dear Jaki,
A quick note to tell you
how much I enjoyed the week-
end — and appreciate all the 1.

22·vij·84
Dear
Jaki,
Many thanks

for your delightful keepsake butterfly and 2.
for the very ki

(Just one more time)

please.... 3.

Dear Jaki —
Thank you SO MUCH for that
great biography. I will run, not
walk, to see the show of the person
with such splendid credentials. 4.

Thanks to: ①Mary Greely, ②Jenny Groat,
③Bill Gunderson, ④Edie Roberts,
⑤Father Philip Waible, ⑥Jan Petrucci,
⑦Awtar Kaur Khalsa
⑧Keith Vinson

& to the many
others who have
written to me.

Before I ask a favor from you, I want
you to know how much I appreciated being 5.

Unfortunately, many
wonderful examples
could not be reproduced
because they were written
in blue ink

#1. I'm interested in running an Italic
Handwriting Column & noticed your 6.

Dear Jaki,
I have used and enjoyed your book "Written Letters"
for quite a few years now. I didn't realize you had
revised it until I peeked into a copy during a recent 7.

Please reserve me a place at the
Quiet time retreat at Menucha. This 8.

A well rounded Calligrapher serves many masters. Letters that are appropriate to one purpose are <u>not</u> always satisfactory for another. Actually, sometimes GREAT HARM is often done the whole Calligraphic movement when a well-meaning but ill-advised student uses the wrong letter at the wrong time. (Uncial on the door to the Ladies' Room?!) One very common mistake has been to use the Italic meant for handwriting for such jobs as menus. Too much information is squeezed into too little space. Usually the distressed Calligrapher must take space from the very important interlinear space in order to get all the copy on the page. (Interlinear space, the space between lines of writing, is necessary for the eye to use to travel from the end of one line of writing back to the beginning of the next line.) When it is too narrow and becomes clogged with tangling & bumping ascenders & descenders the page becomes very difficult to read. Then when the italic is reduced as well, & the thin lines drop out because the printer doesn't know how to "hold" them when making the negative, things get worse. Next the decision is made to print with light brown ink on dark beige paper (so much prettier than black on white, but where's the contrast?) Then the menu is used in a dimly lit restaurant by a customer who's had a couple of drinks & who left his glasses at home. Of course he complains "I can't read this fancy writing!" and stomps out. And what gets the blame? Calligraphy. Any number of things could have helped the situation. Start by choosing an appropriate letterform. (Type might have been best.) If it had to be Italic, use a strong one. If you plan to use your calligraphy commercially, you have a LOT to learn. A good printer can help you a lot, but if he's good, he's probably too busy to conduct classes (unless you are very lucky—as I have been!) Next best, classes in Graphic Reproduction. There are many books on the subject.

See what I mean?

If your writing is going to be reduced photographically & reproduced by multilith you will want to consider some possible variations of form.

MOST, you must understand that learning a few alphabets & falling in love with Calligraphy does not automatically qualify you to become either a commercial artist OR a teacher. Both careers require extensive study.

It's O.K. just to write because you love it & it's a beautiful thing to do. You don't have to make money with it in order to justify it!

* My printer for 20 years has been Morris Boyle. Without his artistry with the camera & the varied skills of his staff at the PHOTO-LITH CO. this book wouldn't have happened.

Mitchell RH 3

To give this version more strength, use about a 40° p.a.

This more formal serif reproduces well.

4 p.w.

I a b c d e

o+b=d

Try to avoid hairlines, especially if you will be having your work reduced.

f g h i j k

k

Where the "ribbon effect" occurs the line should be thin for only an instant, then immediately thicken again.

l m n o p q

'm

'n

start 3 here

P can be left short & straight.

Add or subtract from the length of ascenders &/or descenders as the job requires.

r s t u v w x

r·r

x

Remember, with a lot of copy to read the eye REQUIRES generous interlinear space!

ALTERNATE FORMS.

y z g r t n

This kind of branching eliminates the ribbon effect all together.
If you do any letter this way, do them ALL this way.
Be consistent.

The numerals are surprisingly difficult. This is due, in part, at least, to the subtle differences between the well-made figures & those we have done incorrectly for so long. Another reason is the basic difference in rhythm. These symbols are not western – as are our letter forms. Rather, they are eastern, from India, via Arabia.

Just as the letters were once pictures of things – so were the numbers. The number one is a drawing of one finger. Two is a picture of two fingers held horizontally:

= = = Z = 2

Three: three fingers held horizontally:

= Ξ = Ƶ = 3

(Not two fingers & a stub as 3 would indicate.)

When you do arithmetic it will be least confusing to use the "new style" or "upper case" numbers. These all share common base & top guide lines, thus eliminating the problems caused by tangling ascenders & descenders.

1 2 3 4
5 6 7 8

Can you imagine adding

XXIV
+ XXII
? ? ? ?   Some say that's why the Roman Empire fell!

"New style" or "upper case" numbers are also used when combined with upper case – or majuscule letters:

Four shows a most economical use of line. How much faster + says four than IIII does. + also stands for many very important concepts such as

NORTH
WEST — EAST
SOUTH

RESURRECTION
DEATH — BIRTH
LIFE

Spring – summer – fall – winter

& many more!

113072 TWIGGEN ST.

When upper case figures are used, stretch the 1 2 0 up to the same height as 6 & 8, and bring the rest up to sit on a common base line!

If you are using numbers in combination with minuscule letters, it is most appropriate to use "old style" – or "lower case" numbers which employ ascenders & descenders, as do the minuscule letters.

1130728 Twiggen St.

The join turns + to 4, even tho we do it in 2 strokes: 4. Do keep east strong.

The Romans (who also counted on their fingers) counted five by forming a wedge shape with thumb & fingers:

 = V

but the eastern version shows the five fingers from another aspect:

= 5 ‹ thumb

Be sure to give the numbers plenty of room. They are ruined when crowded.

I don't know where 6 comes from, but recent theory suspects that 7 is a drawing of the seven stars in the big dipper.

8 & 9 remain mysteries.

O is a wonderful, full nothing.

This page was written with a Wm Mitchell Rex nib no. 4

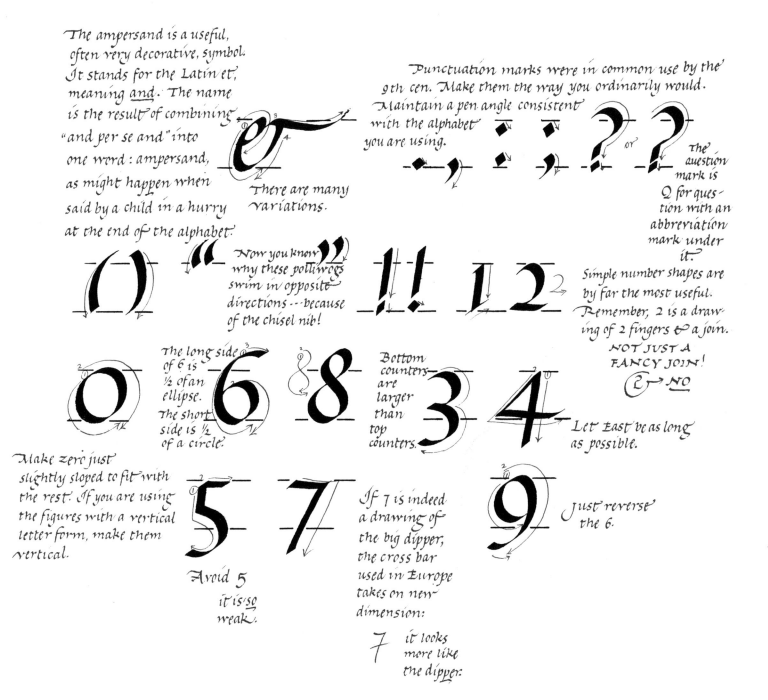

The ampersand is a useful, often very decorative, symbol. It stands for the Latin *et*, meaning <u>and</u>. The name is the result of combining "and per se and" into one word: ampersand, as might happen when said by a child in a hurry at the end of the alphabet.

There are many variations.

Punctuation marks were in common use by the 9th cen. Make them the way you ordinarily would. Maintain a pen angle consistent with the alphabet you are using.

or

The question mark is Q for question with an abbreviation mark under it.

Now you know why these polliwogs swim in opposite directions -- because of the chisel nib!

Simple number shapes are by far the most useful. Remember, 2 is a drawing of 2 fingers & a join. NOT JUST A FANCY JOIN!

NO

The long side of 6 is ½ of an ellipse. The short side is ½ of a circle.

Bottom counters are larger than top counters.

Let East be as long as possible.

Make zero just slightly sloped to fit with the rest. If you are using the figures with a vertical letter form, make them vertical.

Avoid 5 it is <u>so</u> weak.

If 7 is indeed a drawing of the big dipper, the cross bar used in Europe takes on new dimension:

it looks more like the dipper.

Just reverse the 6.

Perhaps it would be useful for you to consider some suggestions I make to my students concerning work habits, attitudes & materials.

To begin, you should know just what you want to achieve. Very often much time is wasted skirting around some hazy notion of the letter form you want to learn. LOOK AT THE MODEL! MEMORIZE IT. Compare your results with the model, and adjust them accordingly. Many students never look back at the model sheet after they once try the letter. Instead they refer to their own letters. What an unfortunate waste of time!

Then understand that there is nothing "gimmicky" about good letters. They happen normally & naturally as a result of good working conditions. The evolution of the letter shapes took place as they were written by PEOPLE LIKE YOU! If you were to write for many hours a day you would have to be comfortable. A twisted or hunched over back gives out too early in the day. A tight, forced hand is too painful

after 45 minutes to allow you to continue. Writing at a slanted table with your chair a good height which allows a straight spine will be very helpful. Your writing arm (if you are righthanded) should be slightly out from your body. Your wrist rests comfortably on its right side. Your fingers are not tense. The forefinger shd be nicely curved so you touch the pen holder with the tip of your finger. The paper should be square in front of you, & the writing should take place just in front of your nose. This means you must learn to move the paper to the left instead of your writing hand to the right as the work progresses. You are not really in control unless the writing takes place right under your nose. The pen angle happens when the above named conditions are met. (Oh, sure, it can be done other ways, but why work any harder than you have to?) The relationship of the tip of the nib to the horizontal guide lines forms the pen angle. Left-handed people achieve the pen angle by turning the paper so its top is parallel to the right side of the table. The left elbow is kept in close to the body as you write. The lack of proper pen angle causes 90% of the problems most people have in learning to write with a flat edged pen, & pen angle is the result of posture. You must be willing to change many old habits.

Pay attention to the letters! Learn to concentrate. This fractured, fragmented world gives us so many concerns that we are usually thinking on several levels at one time. Until you can find some way to empty your mind of everything but the letter your chance of finding the form is slight. Once you have arranged for your physical comfort you must arrange for your mental comfort. Obviously you cannot solve all your problems before picking up your pen each day. So you must learn to put them aside. My students do some simple Yoga exercises at the beginning of each class to help quiet the "monkey mind." If you would like to try a few: Simply stretch! Lift your arms above your head & reach up as far as you can. Then reach out in front as far as possible. With your hands still in front of you grasp the

handles of two imaginary oars and pull back as though rowing a 500 pound boat upstream. Really pull hard. When your fists reach your chest relax - take a deep breath. Straighten your spine. Now, both arms straight out in front again, inhale through your nose until your arms move out straight to each side. Hold your breath while bringing your hands together behind you, lock your thumbs together & exhale while you lift your once again straightened arms as far up as you can. That is so good for relieving the tension in your shoulders. The neck roll is next. Eyes closed (the exercises are all most effective if done with your eyes shut. You'll get into alpha much faster.) slowly rotate your head twice in each direction. Count to 20 on each rotation: one, one thousand, two, one thousand, three, etc. the counting is VERY IMPORTANT, & must be done SLOWLY! Work up to 40. Last - the breathing. Drawing your breath deep down into the lower lobes of your lungs (with your eyes still closed) inhale to the count of 4. Breathe as above. Then exhale 4.

Inhale 4, exhale 6. Inhale 4, exhale 8. Then inhale 4, let you arms drop down to your sides & resume normal breathing while any remaining tension runs out your fingertips. Now you have become still inside. You can become the pen. Become the letter. Become the word. Become the spirit.

Remember that where you are is good. What you do today is for today, & what you do tomorrow is for tomorrow & will be different. As you learn the letters will emerge. Watch them appear without putting value judgements on them or on yourself. As strange as it may seem in the beginning, it will help to resist all connotations of good or bad, right or wrong, praise or blame. Just look at the letters, compare them with the model, & make whatever changes are necessary to conform more to the model.

As soon as possible, do real things. Continuing to just practise month after month, year after year becomes an automatic, meaningless activity. Share the forms (once you know them).

Write out a poem or a weathergram,* preferably your own. Teach a friend.

The materials are many and varied. Simple bond paper, black ink (NOT India or waterproof) a Speedball c-2 nib, a holder, a T-square & a pencil can get you started. Then you can experiment with cutting quill & reed pens & try writing with water color rather than ink. One day you may try vellum & gold. But, whatever you do, remember the basis of the art of Calligraphy is the LETTER. There is no substitute for well made letters, & you will do them well if you practise them well. No amount of fine books or tools can replace the necessary hours & hours of right practise. A good teacher can help, but all a teacher can do is show you the way. Enjoy the going, but expect hills as well as valleys, & beware of tempting plateaus. Take time along the way to enjoy the view.

* Weathergrams are poems of ten words or less. Written on vertical strips of brown kraft paper & hung in the garden or along the trail they are weathered by sun, rain, wind and ice. A weathergram booklet by LJR is available from the Western American Society for Italic Handwriting, 6800 S.E. 32nd St., Portland, Oregon 97202.

WHEN PLANNING THE DESIGN the first consideration must be the function of the finished piece. Calligraphy serves many masters. Lloyd always stood firm in his conviction that the first requirement of the written page is legibility. And, certainly, if the primary function of the work is to convey information, albeit beautifully, he was 100% right. In the present instance, this page wants to talk to you in as comfortable a manner as possible. The lines are short, averaging seven or eight words, the white space between lines of writing is generous enough to allow the eye comfortable passage back to the first of the next line (this consideration is so often overlooked these days by designers attempting to emulate the games being played in the advertising world by people suddenly free from the constraints of old fashioned metal type. Photo type now allows letters to touch & even overlap. And for some purposes, that's great. It is attractive & attention getting, but once you have their attention the message should be clear & easily read.) The words on this page are as close together as possible to help the eye on its journey from left to right, yet not so close that easy differentiation can't take place. It has been found that about the width of the letter n between words works well. Certainly, the distance between lines of writing (called interlinear space) must always be more than the space between words. The interlinear path should not be blocked by tangling ascenders & descenders. To keep the all-important path unblocked I no longer use jots over the i unless it is necessary to avoid possible confusion. Most of the calligraphers in history did not dot the i. The j, however, was born with a jot & requires one. Keep it modest: j, not j. For very short lines used in brief phrases in which the eye & mind get the total message all in one glance, crowding & tangling are permissable.

DECIDE WHAT YOU WANT TO DO Read the copy. Understand it. Let it get into your bones & become part of you. Submerge yourself in it & become it, then you will know what to do. All your understandings of technique will be useless until you can do this. But you must master many techniques if you want to be an artist (& remember, the problems we confront when designing with letters are the same as those encountered in any design problem) There are no short cuts. You will have to study design, drawing, color, watercolor, Art History, & hopefully, modern dance, poetry & literature.

SPACE seems one of the most difficult concepts for most of us to deal with. Possibly because we don't see it. The black line is <u>there</u>, & is so seductive! But, without the white space of the paper, the line would remain unde fined. Lloyd used to say, "Look in your ink bottle! How many letters do you see? They are all there, but you must put the white paper with them." What is true for the letter is true for your design. It cannot ex ist without white space. Learn to look at the unoccupied parts of the page as positive things whose shapes and positions must be considered. The space between the flowers is a flower!

THE PROBLEMS OF LINE are practical ly solved for us by the pen. If you can maintain a pen angle the resulting line is a delight. But don't be blind to the many other possibilities. Play with pointed nibs, flexible nibs, split nibs, pencils, sticks, brushes. These many marks make up the vo cabulary of the artist. Get to know them all.

COLOR is the ongoing study of a life time. Johannes Itten & Joseph Albers can help, but they won't give you

rules. They will help you see. Get some good watercolor (some prefer opaque gouaches), Winsor Newton is good. Learn to fill your nib by stroking it with a paint laden brush. A little gum Arabic will help keep dry paint from smudging. Your color vocabulary will be much richer if you experiment a lot. Black, white & vermilion is the tradi tionally successful color combination, but certainly not the only one.

BALANCE IS BASIC. Sometimes an artist will purposely create imbalance; but it must not happen by accident. If the eye moves too much to one side of the page the design will be out of balance & the viewer will be uncomfortable. You will, of course, respond either positively or negatively to your design if you can turn off your ego & look at the work objectively. Most balance problems are easily solved once you sense that a problem exists. But ego can get in the way & convince you every thing is ok. even when it isn't. That's why we need teachers! No book can make all this clear. Find a class in design!

LOOK AT EXAMPLES. Suddenly there are many wonderful picture books of calli graphy available. Learn by seeing how others have solved problems. Go to ex hibits of all kinds of art.

TU
WXV
XY
Z

1. Encyclopedia Americana, Americana Corp., N.Y. 1958
2. Anderson, Donald M., The Art of Written Forms, Holt, Rinehart & Winston, Inc., N.Y. 1969
3. Baltimore Art Museum, Peabody Institute, Walter's Art Gallery, 2,000 Years of Calligraphy, 1965
4. Barnard, Mary, Sappho, Univ. of Ca. Press, Berkeley, '60
5. Benson, John Howard, The First Writing Book (Arrighi's Operina), Yale Univ., New Haven, 1959
6. Camp, Ann, Pen Lettering, Dryad, G.B. 1978
7. Catich, E.M., The Origin of the Serif, The Catfish Press, St. Ambrose Coll., Davenport, Iowa, '68
8. Catich, E.M., The Trajan Inscription in Rome, Catfish Press, St. Ambrose Coll., Davenport, Iowa, 1961
9. Degering, Hermann, Lettering, Taplinger/Pentalic, New York City, N.Y. 1978
10. Da Boll, Raymond, Recollections of the Lyceum & Chatauqua Circuits, Bond Wheelwright Co., Freeport, Maine. 1969
11. Dair, Carl, Design With Type, U. of Toronto 1967
12. Dawson, Giles, Elizabethan Handwriting, Faber & Faber, London, 1966
13. Dubay, Inga & Getty, Barbara, Italic Handwriting Series, P.S.U., Portland, Ore., 1980
14. Fairbank, Alfred, A Book of Scripts, Penguin, '55
15. Fairbank, Alfred, A Handwriting Manual, Faber & Faber, London 1964
16. Gelb, I.J., A Study of Writing, U. of Chicago, 1963
17. Gütler, Andre, The Development of the Roman Alphabet, Basle
18. Harvard, Stephen, An Italic Copybook, The Cataneo Manuscript, Taplinger/Pentalic, New York City, New York 1981
19. Hewitt, Graily, Lettering, Seely, Service & Co., Ltd., London 1954
20. Hunter, Dard, My Life With Paper, Borzoi Books, New York City, N.Y. 1958
21. Jackson, Donald, The Story of Writing, Taplinger/Pentalic, New York 1981
22. Johnston, Edward, Formal Penmanship & Other Papers, edited by Heather Child, Taplinger/Pentalic, New York
23. Johnston, Edward, Writing, Lettering & Illuminating, Pitman, New York 1958
26. Johnston, Priscilla, Edward Johnston, Taplinger/Pentalic, New York, N.Y. 1976
25. Kindersley, David, & Cardozo, Lida Lopez, Letters Slate Cut, Taplinger/Pentalic, N.Y. 1981
26. Lamb, C.M., The Calligrapher's Handbook, Faber & Faber, London
27. Lindegren, Eric, ABC of Lettering, Eric Lindegren Grafisk Studio, Askim, Sweden 1964
28. Lindegren, Eric, An ABC Book, Pentalic, N.Y.
29. Mahoney, Dorothy, The Craft of Calligraphy, Taplinger/Pentalic, New York 1982
30. Mason, John, Paper Making, Faber & Faber, London 1959
31. Nemoy, Maury, The Study of Letterforms, The Scorpio Press 1964
32. Ogg, Oscar, Three Classics of Italian Calligraphy, Arrighi, Tagliente & Palatino, Dover '53
33. Osley, A.S., Calligraphy, & Palaeography, Faber & Faber, London 1965
34. Osley, A.S., Luminario, Nieukoop, Miland 1972
35. Osley, A.S., Scribes & Sources, D.R. Godine 1980
36. Pearce, Charles, The Little Manual of Calligraphy, Taplinger/Pentalic, N.Y. 1981
37. Portland Art Museum, Calligraphy. It's Golden Age & Modern Revival 1958
38. Reynolds, Lloyd, Italic Calligraphy, Taplinger/Pentalic Corp., New York 1969
39. Standard, Paul, Calligraphy's Flowering, Decay & Restauration, Taplinger/Pentalic 1981
40. Stern, Jess, Yoga, Youth & Reincarnation, Bantam '68
41. Suzuki, S., Zen Mind, Beginner's Mind, Weatherhill '72
42. Svaren, J., Lojor's Letters, TBW Books, Woolwich, Ma. '81
43. Thompson, Sir Edward Maunde, An Introduction to Greek & Latin Palaeography, Ares Publishers, Inc., Chicago, Illinois
44. Tschichold, Jan, An Illustrated History of Writing & Lettering, Col. U. Press, N.Y. '66
45. Ullman, Berthold, Ancient Writing & Its Influence, Cooper Square Pub, N.Y. 1963
46. Wardrop, James, The Script of Humanism, Oxford at the Clarendon Press 1963
47. Whalley, Joyce Irene, The Pen's Excellencie, Taplinger/Pentalic, New York 1980

In 1975 Alfred Fairbank wrote of Written Letters, "Your book is fascinating, feminine, honest & Oregonian." The "Oregonian" part worried me. When I asked Lloyd what he thought A.F. meant he answered, "We have begun to develop a distinct style of Calligraphy here in Oregon." At the time that seemed fine to me. Few reference books were available to me; & almost no original work, other than that done locally.

As time passed more & more beautiful books were published. Thousands of Americans became enthralled with beautiful letters & began to invite fine teachers to come & share ideas with us. It became possible for me to travel and see more. The results of all this have been growth & change. I am still very proud of what is happening in Oregon. However, I hope the changes you will find in some of the letter forms make them a bit less regional.

I will doubtless wish for the strength & opportunity to make further changes in the future.

J.S.
2/1/82